BP Book of MOTOR

1350

7s. 6d. net

MOTOR RACING

Edited by MAXWELL BOYD

STANLEY PAUL *London*

STANLEY PAUL & CO. LTD
178-202 Great Portland Street, London, W.1

AN IMPRINT OF THE   HUTCHINSON GROUP

London Melbourne Sydney
Auckland Bombay Toronto
Johannesburg New York

First published 1959

*This book has been set in Plantin type face.
It has been printed in Great Britain by
Litho Offset at Taylor Garnett Evans &
Co. Ltd., Watford, Herts., and bound by them*

ABOUT THIS BOOK

JUAN FANGIO WRITES:

Motor racing is a young sport predominantly for the young, and although I have had, regretfully, to retire as a racing driver, I make a point of giving support to anything that will increase enthusiasm among young men and women who are interested either as spectators or as participants. This is why I commend the BP Book of Motor Racing, since I am sure that it will stimulate interest and draw people to the circuits all over the world. Like all sports, motor racing depends for survival on the well-informed enthusiast, and the more books like this one we have, the brighter the future will be.

Many people tell me that motor racing is at the crossroads, that important decisions about the size of cars and circuits must be taken, and indeed have been taken, and that the next few years may be years of decreasing popularity. For my part, since I do not think anything will stop the sport becoming more and more suited to the tastes of our modern mechanized age, I look forward to the future with excitement and interest, and, if you are wise enough to make a hobby of following or competing in motor racing, you will frequently see me at international circuits in my new role of enthusiastic *aficionado*.

STIRLING MOSS SAYS:

International motor racing, the subject of this book, must watch out for itself during the next few years. For, after riding on the crest of an ever-growing wave of popularity since the war, a critical time is approaching.

Grand Prix motor racing is a spectacle sport and relies on the continued and large-scale support of the public for its livelihood.

Recently the international authorities in charge of the sport have been falling over backwards in a somewhat misplaced effort to make motor racing safer by cutting down speeds. This has resulted in the 1961 Formula 1 of $1\frac{1}{2}$-litres. Now, this limitation of engine capacity may make Grand Prix racing a little slower for a time. But I don't think it will necessarily make it any safer.

The only thing I am certain it will do is to take away much of the spectacle value of the game by reducing speeds and by forcing the building of smaller and smaller cars. And if the spectacle in Grand Prix racing is going to be lacking, then so will be the crowds coming to see it. If motor racing suddenly finds itself out in the cold after 1961, it only has C.S.I. to blame.

Contents

Acknowledgements

Grateful thanks are due to the following sources for their permission to reproduce the illustrations used in this book:

The British Petroleum Company Limited; Edward Eves; John Ross; Maxwell Boyd, A.I.B.P.; Autosport; Giovanni Lurani; Rootes Motors Limited; The Nuffield Organization; P.A.-Reuter; Publifoto; Dr. Ing. h.c. F. Porsche K.G.; Central Press.

Monza

1 This is Motor Racing

MOTOR racing is the sport of the twentieth century. The sport of speed, of glamour, of knife-edge judgment and split-second reaction. Of men pitting themselves and the machines they have created against each other and the forces of nature. That's how the more romantically-minded see it. And that is basically what it is, although dyed-in-the-wool racing men might pooh-pooh the idea with embarrassment.

Why do men go motor racing? You might as well ask why they climb mountains, or go potholing, or do anything at all which has an element of danger about it. If you asked the drivers themselves, you would probably get an odd variety of answers, none of which would give you a great deal of satisfaction.

One might say, 'because I like it'. Another, 'because that is the way I earn my living'. A third, 'because of the kick it gives me'. A fourth, 'because it is my sport just as football might be anyone else's', and a fifth, 'I haven't the faintest idea. I just do!'

Not very rewarding replies, perhaps, but that is not because the drivers were trying to be lofty or secretive about it. You go motor racing because it is a challenge, and human nature cannot resist a challenge, whether it is to a game of shove ha'penny or to a battle royal. You also do it because you like it. And one thing every racing driver would be at pains to point out is, 'we don't *have* to do it, you know. It's up to us.'

So let us leave it at that, shall we? We think motor racing is the greatest sport in the world. And if you are not already converted, we hope you will be by the time you have finished this book. Well, not converted, perhaps. That is a lot to ask one small book to do. Let us say we hope we shall have told you enough about the sport to whet your appetite and make you want to go and find out for yourself what motor racing is all about. As for you, the enthusiast, we hope the book will help you to increase your enjoyment of motor racing and give you some pleasant and perhaps useful reading.

How It All Started

The first motor race of all took place on Sunday, 22 July, 1894, between Paris and Rouen, a distance of some eighty miles. The event was sponsored by a far-sighted Paris newspaper as a demonstration of the capabilities of the revolutionary, new horseless carriage. As such, it was not at first intended to be a race. But prizes were offered for those arriving at Rouen, so it turned into one quite easily.

Twenty-one cars took part, some famous names amongst them—Panhard, Peugeot, De Dion and Benz—and all were petrol- or

steam-powered. But other odd forms of propulsion, such as gravity, compressed air, pedals and high-pressure gas were used by other entrants whose cars failed to pass the race qualification tests.

Later that same Sunday, six hours and forty-eight minutes after leaving Paris to be precise, Count De Dion was the first to arrive at Rouen. He was mounted on a steam tractor of his own design and towing some friends in a carriage. He averaged 11·6 m.p.h. for the 78·5-mile run. However, this odd vehicle did not comply with the spirit of the regulations, as they say, being more of a traction engine than a horseless carriage. So the first prize of £200 was divided between the Peugeot and Panhard petrol-powered cars which finished soon after him and which carried all their passengers in the approved manner on the machine itself.

The idea of racing these extraordinary beasts called motor cars caught the public imagination immediately. And the cars' builders and drivers saw in racing an excellent way of publicising the vehicles and over-coming the considerable opposition to them.

Between 1895 and 1900 there followed a series of races from city to city which would be considered marathons today, let alone over sixty years ago. Paris-Bordeaux-Paris (732 miles), Paris-Marseilles-Paris (1,062 miles), Paris-Amsterdam-Paris (890 miles), and the first Tour de France which covered a distance of 1,350 miles. Remember, these were races, not rallies, in the most primitive of vehicles and the feats of sheer will-power and human endeavour they provoked are exhausting just to read about in these days of such engineering refinements as four-wheel brakes, shock absorbers and steering wheels. For example, there was the great Emile Levassor's epic run in the Paris-Bordeaux-Paris race of 1895 when the Frenchman sat at the tiller (!) of

Jack Fairman at Goodwood in 1959, Maseratimounted for the first time

American drivers are making their mark on the European scene. This is Masten Gregory in a Cooper

Sports cars use all the road—and more—after a Le Mans-type start at Silverstone

his Panhard for over forty-eight hours, driving the car the entire distance single-handed, stopping only for fuel, oil and water. And Levassor beat the man in second place by about six hours!

In November 1896 came the famous Emancipation Run from London to Brighton, which is still commemorated each year by the popular veteran car run over the same route. This was no race, but it marked a milestone in British motoring by celebrating the Highways Act of that year. This Act gave the motor car the freedom of the road (but only a 12 m.p.h. freedom), and did away with the man who used to have to walk in front of each car to give the frightened population warning of its impending and dangerous approach.

To return to motor racing. These early and gigantic 'round trips' from Paris were supported wholly by Continental cars until 1899, when the Hon. Scott-Montagu entered his Daimler in the Paris-Ostend race.

Also in 1899 there occurred a very odd race indeed of about 100 miles between Paris and Trouville. Racing cars were pitted against motor cyclists, cyclists, horses and pedestrians, the whole thing being worked out on an elaborate handicapping system. For instance, the footsloggers were given twenty hours for the race against the racing cars' three hours. The event was won by a horse.

Back in Britain the motor car was still thought of as an invention of a particularly vengeful Devil. However, a good deal of the country-wide opposition had been overcome three years earlier by the 1,000 Miles Trial of 1900, organized by the R.A.C. to demonstrate to the nation that the motor car was something more than a dangerous, dust-raising toy. It was actually the choking clouds of dust kicked up by the cars on the dry, unmade roads that was the basic cause of their unpopularity, not their noise or speed.

Over in France in 1900 the first of the famous Gordon Bennett series of races took place, sponsored by the rich and enthusiastic owner of the *New York Herald*. This covered 350 miles, was won by Fernand Charron and, as each following year's race was to take place in the country of the previous year's winner, the 1901 Gordon Bennett event went to France again.

Only one driver, a Frenchman, finished on this occasion. But the following year a magnificent victory was scored by an Englishman, S. F. Edge, one of the greatest racing drivers of his day, at the wheel of a Napier. At last Britain and her motor industry were making themselves felt in international motor-racing circles, up to now dominated by the French.

According to the rules, the 1903 race for the Gordon Bennett Trophy should have been held in England. But the very thought of holding a race for these dirty, noisy, dusty monsters on the fair roads of England, even on a controlled circuit, horrified the authorities then, as it still does nearly sixty years later. They believed that no gentleman should travel by anything but horsepower, and that should be generated by real horses. The speed limit was 12 m.p.h. and there it would stay. Not even a racing car would be allowed to exceed the legal rate. So the race was run in Ireland, where everyone supported the idea wholeheartedly and where they still close the roads for motor races to this very day.

The event took place over a long circuit south of Dublin and was won by a German, Camille Jenatzy, driving a 60 h.p. Mercedes. This vehicle was actually no more than a hurriedly prepared, tuned-up touring car, as the entire team of three Mercedes racing cars were destroyed by fire on the eve of the race.

Meanwhile, the gigantic city-to-city races which had continued during the first years of the new century, had come to a sticky end. The last of them was Paris-Madrid in 1902, this race being stopped by the authorities at

Hawthorn heads the queue in an
Italian Grand Prix at Monza

Bordeaux after several cars had been involved in fatal accidents with uncontrolled crowds of spectators. Thereafter racing on unguarded roads was banned in France. Fifty-five years later the same fate befell the Italian classic, the Mille Miglia, for the same reason. There is nothing new in motor racing.

France ran the first French Grand Prix over a 65-mile circuit outside Le Mans. This was the first race of the Grand Prix era, in which engine size has continually decreased as power has continually increased, and of which our World Championship events today are direct descendants.

Successor to the ill-fated V16 car is the current 2½-litre BRM

By 1904 the basis of racing car design was changing. Up to that time the only way of finding more speed had been to increase the size of the engine and lighten the chassis. Now the limit had been reached and chassis frames were crumpling under the weight of the engine and the strain of the power it gave. From this point on, smaller engines were made to work harder to produce the same amount and more power.

In June 1906, the Automobile Club of

The story of half a century of Grand Prix racing is long, involved and tremendously exciting—but, unfortunately, too long, to tell here. It covers triumph and disaster. Cars which swept all before them, overcoming all opposition, and those which should have done so but failed dismally. And it covers the work of the engineers whose constant search for yet more power and speed, coupled with those often elusive qualities, controllability and reliability, has resulted in racing cars about one-eighth the size of the

Above: *Pre-war simplicity (Mercedes-Benz)*

Below: *Post-war complexity (Maserati)*

1906 models travelling at speeds approaching 200 m.p.h.

But before we leave the pioneering age of motor competitions, one fantastic event deserves mention. This was a race from New York to Paris in 1908, promoted by the French newspaper *Le Matin*, who had previously organized a Pekin-Paris run.

Motor Racing Today

International motor racing today is divided into seven categories, all of which have their rules, regulations and limitations. The sport is run strictly 'according to the book'. And the book has many, many pages of what you can do and what you cannot do.

Formula 1. This is the Grand Prix Formula to which all events counting for the Drivers' World Championship are run. Many other races, some of them with the title of Grand Prix, others without, are also run to this Formula each year. It specifies that cars raced to the Formula must have a supercharged engine with a cubic capacity not exceeding 750 c.c., or an unsupercharged engine not exceeding 2,500 c.c. There are no restrictions on minimum or maximum weight, but in each instance the fuel used must be aviation petrol.

Formula 2. This is basically intended as the 'advanced training school' for drivers intending, or hoping, to enter full-scale Grand Prix racing. It calls for cars with unsupercharged engines not exceeding 1,500 c.c. and running on aviation fuel.

Formula 3. Although this is still an International Formula, to all intents and purposes it is supported only by Britain. Formula 3 races of International status are no longer organized by the rest of Europe. Here car engines are restricted to a maximum of 500 c.c. unsupercharged.

Formula Junior. This recent Formula was devised by the Italians for much the same reasons as Britain devised Formula 3 shortly after the war—namely to encourage the building of cheap single-seater racing cars, and to make it easier and less expensive for up-and-coming drivers to enter the sport. The latter consideration is especially important to Italy, the ranks of whose top racing drivers have shrunk almost to nil in recent years.

Formula Junior racing cars are single-seater vehicles with a mechanical basis built from parts of a recognized production touring car of which at least 1,000 must have been made in twelve consecutive months. Other requirements are: minimum wheelbase, 200 cm. (6 ft. 8 in.); minimum track, 110 cm. (3 ft. 8 in.); maximum overall width of body, 95 cm. (3 ft. 2 in.) and minimum weight, 400 kg. (a little under 8 cwt.). There are various other requirements on the mechanical side, affecting such things as the cylinder block and head, the gearbox, the braking system and the carburation. The fuel specified is premium grade pump petrol.

Formule Libre. This is not an official International Formula. It merely means 'Free Formula', or simply, 'anything goes'. And many races of this nature, where the types of cars entered are simply left to the discretion of the organizers, are run each year. This happens particularly in the farther-flung corners of the globe where there are insufficient cars of any one type to make a race to a particular Formula. Here you get racing cars, ordinary sports cars and all kinds of home-built 'specials' lumped together in an always interesting, sometimes spectacular, event.

Sports Cars. The engines of cars competing for the World Sports Car Championship must not exceed 3,000 c.c. in capacity. In addition, they must comply with various other requirements mainly concerning the bodywork. These have been laid down primarily to keep thinly disguised single-

The tail wags the dog at Brands Hatch. Ian Burgess's Cooper with extreme oversteer

seater racing cars out of sports car events. For instance, each vehicle must have two front seats, one each side of its centre line, and they must be built and placed in the car according to given dimensions.

Sports cars of more than 500 c.c. must have two doors of a given minimum size (one each side, it is carefully pointed out!). The wings of all cars must be solid with the body and must surround at least one-third of the circumference of the road wheel. A safety-glass windscreen must be used, plus an electric windscreen wiper. Other 'musts' are a self-starter, a rear mirror, a spare wheel carried so that it does not get in the way of the passengers or the doors, an efficient silencer (and they define what they mean by 'efficient') and a hood, although this only has to be produced for the scrutineer's inspection. And just to make sure that nobody gets away with anything, just about every bodywork item has its minimum or maximum measurement, down to the nearest centimetre. These regulations,

incidentally, are contained in full in Appendix C of the International Sporting Code of the F.I.A.

Touring Cars. The regulations concerning Touring and Grand Touring Cars in saloon car races and rallies are sub-divided into six groups concerning normal cars, improved series production cars and special cars in each category. The rules are somewhat lengthy and complicated, and are contained in full in Appendix J of the International Sporting Code.

Formula 1, 1961. A new Grand Prix Formula comes into force on 1 January, 1961. It calls for cars with a cubic capacity not exceeding 1,500 c.c. unsupercharged, weighing at least 500 kg. (9·8 cwt.), and running on the best available premium pump grade fuel. In addition, an automatic starter must be fitted, and fuel tanks must be of the flexible aircraft safety type, to lessen the likelihood of the tank bursting and blazing in an accident. The bodywork must not enclose

19

the cockpit or the wheels, an anti-roll bar must be fitted to protect the driver should the car overturn and there must be a separate emergency braking system working on the two front wheels at least. Finally, no car may take on additional oil during the race. This lessens the likelihood of oil being spilled on the track.

These various Formulae and racing regulations are laid down by the Fédération de l'Automobile (F.I.A.). For further information about this organization, see Chapter 7, page 93.

The Grand Prix Formulae are given on page 18.

Championships

Each year the F.I.A. awards five Championships for International speed events.

World Championship of Drivers

The title of World Champion Driver goes to the driver making the six best performances in the annual list of 'classic' and other Grand Prix races drawn up by the International Sporting Commission (C.S.I.) of the F.I.A. If less than ten events are run, then the driver's five best placings count, or four best placings if there are only five events. If there should be less than five events by any chance, the Championship is cancelled.

In 1959 the following events counted for the World Championship of Drivers:

10 May	Grand Prix of Monaco.
30 May	500 Miles of Indianapolis.
31 May	Grand Prix of Holland.
14 June	Grand Prix of Belgium.
5 July	Grand Prix of France.
18 July	British Grand Prix.
2 August	Grand Prix of Germany.
23 August	Grand Prix of Portugal.
13 September	Grand Prix of Italy.
11 October	Grand Prix of Morocco.
12 December	Grand Prix of the U.S.A.

The French Grand Prix also took the title of Grand Prix of Europe 1959.

Events counting for the Championship occasionally vary from year to year, but the list for 1960 is likely to be similar to that given above.

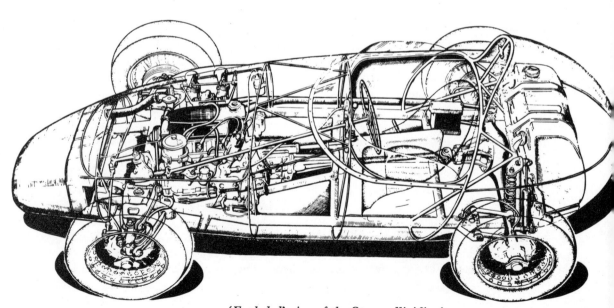

'Exploded' view of the Stanguellini Junior shows the general layout of the new Formula Junior cars

The Raineri is representative of Formula Junior cars. At the wheel at Monaco: Fangio's protégé Juan Manuel Bordeu

All events in this Championship must cover a minimum distance of 300 km. (186½ miles) and last for a minimum of two hours. They are run to the requirements of Formula I, with the exception of the Indianapolis 500 which has its own American formula.

Championship points are awarded as follows: To the driver of the car in 1st place —8 points; 2nd place—6 points; 3rd place—4 points; 4th place—3 points; 5th place—2 points. The driver making the fastest lap in each race receives an additional point. This is divided equally if more than one driver makes the same time on the fastest lap. In the event of a tie at the end of the season, second and third placings in events are taken into consideration in deciding the Championship title. No changing of drivers is allowed during a World Championship race. If a car retires, the driver retires with it as far as win or place points are concerned. He can no longer climb into a team mate's car, finish in a place and share the first driver's points.

International Championship of Sports Cars

One important point to begin with—this is a Championship for makes of cars, not for drivers.

In this case the C.S.I. names the makes of car which they will allow to compete in the Championship, as well as naming the races which will count towards it. These events must cover a minimum distance of 1,000 km. (620 miles), or last at least six hours. If circumstances make it unavoidable that they cover a lesser distance of between 650 km. and 1,000 km., or last only between four and six hours, the points awarded are halved.

In 1959 the following events counted for Sports Car Championship:

21 March	Twelve Hours of Sebring.
24 May	Targa Florio.
7 June	Thousand Kilometres of Nürburgring.
20/21 June	Twenty-Four Hours of Le Mans.
5 September	Tourist Trophy.

The Championship goes to the make of car making the six best performances in ten to twelve races; five best in six to nine races, or four best out of five races. Less than five races means the cancellation of the Championship. Ties are decided by taking second placings into consideration.

Championship points are awarded as follows: To the make of car in 1st place—8 points; 2nd place—6 points; 3rd place—4 points; 4th place—3 points; 5th place—2 points. Points are given only to those cars

21

entered with the manufacturer's permission, and which have the best placings in the general classification. Thus, if a car of the same marque as the winner is placed anywhere from second to fifth, it does not gain extra points. There is no extra point award for the car making the fastest lap.

Constructors' Championship, Formula 1

This Championship is awarded on a points basis to the make of car putting up the best performance in the same series of races as that counting for the Drivers' Championship. Points are awarded as follows: 1st place—8 points; 2nd place—6 points; 3rd place—4 points; 4th place—3 points; 5th place—2 points.

Constructors' Championship, Formula 2

Awarded on points to the make of car putting up the best performance in the series of International Formula 2 events drawn up annually by the C.S.I.

Points are awarded as follows: 1st place—8 points; 2nd place—6 points; 3rd place—4 points; 4th place—3 points; 5th place—2 points.

International Hillclimb Championship

This is a drivers' championship, but one which hardly affects Britain. Because we lack a suitable venue, all the events take place on the Continent where they have hill-climbs which wind onwards and upwards for miles. In 1959 the Championship hillclimbs were these:

28 June	Mont Ventoux, France.
4 July	Pike's Peak, U.S.A.
12 July	Trento-Bondone, Italy.
28 July	Fribourg, Germany.
15 August	Gaisberg, Austria.
29/30 August	Hillclimb Grand Prix, Switzerland.

The regulations state that each hillclimb must have a minimum run of 6 km. (3·72 miles) and must rise by a given amount between the start and finish. Competing cars are limited to a capacity of 1,500 c.c. and must be sports cars conforming to the requirements of Appendix C of the International Sporting Code. Four best placings count out of five events, four out of six to nine events and six out of ten or more events. Points: 1st place—8 points; 2nd place—6 points; 3rd place—4 points; 4th place—3 points; 5th place—2 points.

Going Motor Racing

So you want to become a racing driver? Well, that's not unreasonable. And it is not too difficult to achieve either, providing you don't set your sights too high at first.

The first thing you need, obviously, is a car. It does not have to be something long, sleek and glamorous like a Lotus, or an Elva or a Cooper. Unless you can afford it. But even if something like that is within your bank balance, you would be much better advised to make your first tottering steps in competition motoring in something less powerful and more manageable. These modern sports/racing cars are fast and frisky. In practised hands they are race winners alright, but to a beginner they can be a terrible handful. They are G.C.E. standard and you are only in kindergarten—remember?

So settle for an ordinary sports car. A second-hand one possibly, say an M.G. TD or something like that. Oh yes, you can get into a lot of trouble even with an M.G. if you are not too careful, but it will keep you out of a great deal more. Anyway, some people could get into trouble driving a pram.

But, as your racing car may have to be your business and shopping car as well, you may not want anything as sporty as an M.G., especially in our climate. Right. There are plenty of races for saloon cars; hillclimbs and sprints as well. More than one somewhere in Britain every weekend. So you certainly will not be out of it if you are stuck with the bread-and-butter family saloon. Or even with an estate car or small van for that matter. You can see them performing very creditably at many of the smaller meetings these days.

The alternative to buying a car is, of course, doing-it-yourself—building your own special. But that rather depends on the extent of your mechanical know-how, although one prominent manufacturer of sports/racing cars now sells his 'junior' model in a kit complete with instructions. A screwdriver and a couple of spanners and you are away! All the same, this is by far the cheapest way of getting yourself on to a circuit. But the cheapest of the lot is to pick up bits and pieces here and there, from breakers' yards and so on, and string them all together in the back yard. But as we said, you need to know what you are doing. You must satisfy the scrutineers before they will let you race, and they are a hard-headed bunch of automobile engineers. They will not let your machine out, however fast, if it looks as though it is lashed together with sticky tape.

What if you cannot afford a car at all? Well, there is a scheme in existence where cars from a central pool are hired out to drivers for races. But a certain standard of driving ability is called for rather naturally. If you are a raw recruit to the game and cannot afford a car, then the only thing to do is to try to borrow one from a friend (easier said than done admittedly), or just resign yourself to watching. Many people spend their time watching and have just as much fun as the drivers on the circuit.

For the luckier ones though—having got

Ecurie Ecosse Jaguars have won twice at Le Mans. This is Ron Flockhart at the wheel

your car and prepared it for the job, the next thing is to find somewhere to race it. Join a recognized motoring club (if you have not already done so), one that either organizes its own race meetings, or is invited to take part in other clubs' meetings. There are scores of them—meetings and clubs—and a glance through the R.A.C. Fixture List will find them. The club you choose will also no doubt run sprints and hillclimbs and driving tests as well, and these will give you good practice at the wheel.

You will also need a Competition Licence from the R.A.C. Incidentally, this will not let you drive in a Grand Prix, or anything like that, straight away. You have to work your way up these days, qualifying by racing, from a 'junior' to a 'senior' licence, so to speak.

After two or three seasons of club meetings on circuits all over the country, you will probably be wondering where you go from there. If you have shown above average talent, you may already have been asked to drive something considerably faster than your original car. You may also have taken a course at one of the excellent racing driving schools now running. There is the Cooper Car Company's training school at Brands Hatch, and Jim Russell's at Snetterton, for instance. If you do have talent, they will find it. And once you have graduated you will have the experience necessary to take you to more powerful machinery.

From this point you can work your way up to National meetings, then International ones. After that the sky (and the World Championship) is the limit. Because if you are good you will be noticed. Factory team talent spotting for potential Grand Prix drivers goes on all the time.

But there is no short cut. The only way to become a 'works'—or Grand Prix driver—or any kind of racing driver at all for that matter is—GET A CAR AND DRIVE!

Snack for a champion's wife while the champion is out racing. Katie Moss at Rheims

24

Stirling Moss driving Rob Walker's 2½-litre Cooper-Climax at Zandvoort

*Sports cars lined up
on the grid at Aintree*

A Ferrari follows a BRM
'round the houses' at Monte Carlo
during the Monaco Grand Prix, 1959

Petrol and oil. You drive into your garage, fill up with a few gallons of one and a pint or so of the other. The only time you really ever think about them is when they run out and you are stranded. You have confidence in them, and you take them for granted. You know they will do their job properly. The oil will save your engine from harm, saving your money at the same time, and the petrol will make the car give all the power it can. And a good deal of the credit for this is due to motor racing.

Big-time motor racing is the roughest, toughest school in the world—for drivers, for cars and for the things that make cars tick. It is the hardest, most testing research ground there is. Disc brakes started on racing cars. Soon they will be fitted to most family saloons as well. Those far more efficient headlights fitted to your new car—they result from the experience of drivers trying to keep up a race average in the slashing rain at night at Le Mans. Nearly everything your car is made of owes something to motor racing research.

So it is with oil. The mechanical side of the modern racing car works tremendously hard. Those small engines produce so much power that the stresses and strains are fantastic. Each year new, lighter and stronger metals are used, but they would all be useless if it was not for the oil that keeps them going. The oil that literally keeps them apart. Only a thin, almost invisible film of oil separates the moving parts of racing engines and transmissions, turning over hour after hour, thousands of times each minute and strained to the limit. And that film must never break.

The scientists must develop lubricating oils that will stand the strain. And they must go on improving them to keep pace with racing engine design, which is always leaps and bounds ahead of production engine design. So the oil people know that when they have developed a product that works faultlessly in a racing car, they have learned lessons they can apply to improving the oil in ordinary cars.

So the next time you tip a pint of oil into the engine of your family saloon, remember that much of the reason why it does its job so well is because it was probably developed, tried and tested in battle on the motor racing circuits of the world.

Roy Salvadori (Aston Martin) spinning during the Tourist Trophy race, Goodwood, 1958. He drove on to finish second

29

Left: *The rich colours of motor racing—Maseratis at Monza*

2 *The 'Big Six' Drivers*

JUAN MANUEL FANGIO

TWENTY-TWO years ago the great French driver Jean Pierre Wimille saw a young mechanic drive a home-built Ford Special in a minor race in the Argentine. Wimille recognized talent when he saw it. 'Brilliant,' he said, 'the day he has a real car to drive, he will perform miracles!'

The driver was Juan Manuel Fangio. His age was twenty-six. Twenty-one years later he was a national hero, and had been crowned World Champion five times in seven years.

What is he like, this Supremo who made his first European appearance (Rheims, 1948) aged thirty-seven—an age when others in the game are thinking of leaving it? Is he our idea of a champion of a tough sport? Big, brawny, strong, silent and remote?

The opposite is the truth. Now almost fifty and retired, he looks like a prosperous, lively business man. He would be lost in a crowd. He has nothing of the virtuoso's showmanship, and his voice resembles a gramophone record played backwards fast. His countrymen call him 'El Chueco'—the bandy-legged one.

But his eyes are needle-sharp and diamond-bright. Eyes that helped perform the prophesied miracles, helped him become the highest exponent of the art of motor racing. In the language of today, Juan Manuel Fangio was 'the greatest'. He may have retired, but our memories of him have not.

Talking to his Argentine protégé, Juan Manuel Bordeu, at Monte Carlo

On the limit with a Maserati at Rouen

STIRLING MOSS

Here is a man who has an answer for everything. You've got to be up early in the morning (which he never is, if he can help it) to catch out Stirling Moss. For here is a professional professional. A man dedicated to the sport which is his business.

Moss goes into each motor race as a clever businessman goes into the conference room. Physically and mentally alert, having sized up the opposition, anticipated their moves and knowing in advance exactly what line he must take in order to win the day. He always expects the unexpected and a fast one has to be pulled very fast indeed if it is to make any impression on his organized, calculating mind.

But there is no conference room equivalent of a mechanical breakdown in a motor race. There is no counter to it either. It is a complete and utter end to the job in hand and can only be answered philosophically or temperamentally. Moss chooses the former course, and as someone remarked when his brilliant drive in the 1959 Monaco Grand Prix ended abruptly with a crunch of metal, 'Poor bloke—he can't even go and drown his sorrows in a bottle!' For in the season, Moss does not drink and hardly smokes at all. And his 'season' lasts virtually twelve months in every year. A spartan life? Perhaps. But which of us wouldn't put up with the same for an annual income which would keep two Prime Ministers at Downing Street?

Moss is on the short side and successful. And it is one of the most popular misconceptions that such people should necessarily be swollen-headed. Of Moss this is simply not true. He is not self-effacing or retiring— why should he be? He is a showman in a showman's business. But he has no greater opinion of himself and his achievements than they merit. He always has time for other people and things—provided the time is not going to be wasted.

He must always be active, doing something which seems, to him at any rate, to have a purpose—even if it is only playing cards for a whole plane journey when he could be reading, or just sleeping. He is quite intolerant of inefficiency, inactivity and imperfection. Life with Moss is exhausting. One is continually 'on the go'. Ask his wife, Katie. She knows better than any.

Moss in the Vanwall at Zandvoort on the way to winning the Dutch Grand Prix 1958

MIKE HAWTHORN

Mike Hawthorn, Britain's first World Champion Driver, was an Englishman's idea of an English sportsman. He dressed in a tweed jacket or a sober grey suit. He liked his pipe and his pint of bitter. He wore a battered old cap. He kept a dog. His only concession to showmanship was his bow-tie 'trade mark'. Although he did not ignore the hard cash side of his racing, the game was first and foremost to him a sport. And as he realized its dangers, he gave it up at the peak of his fame. He could understand the outlook of other, more professionally-minded drivers, but could never subscribe to it. 'It's their job,' he would say, 'but mine's running a garage.'

Mike was a 'natural'. Driving an elderly Riley Sprite, he won his first race, in Ireland, in June 1951. Two years later he beat Fangio himself after a hell-for-leather battle to win the Grand Prix of France. He went up like a rocket, but found life at the top could be tough.

Over National Service he was subjected to a blast of adverse criticism. And Mike unfortunately never learned to ignore unkind criticism. He was too easily hurt. Sometimes, too, he offended other people, for he was, like all great artists, temperamental. He took a great deal of knowing. But once one understood him, no one could be kinder nor more helpful.

Mike took a great deal of notice of those friends of his who also raced motor cars. He helped them in every way he could, often accompanying them to races to watch and offer on-the-spot advice. But here tragedy stepped in. Not long after his father died in a road accident, his protégé, Mike Currie, was also killed. Later, another close friend, Don Beauman, met his death while racing. It is surprising the effect of these tragedies was not greater.

But, no. Mike went on racing more brilliantly than ever to end by reaching the highest peak of all. For many years to come the toast will be—Mike Hawthorn, Englishman, sportsman, World Champion!

Hawthorn at Zandvoort driving the Ferrari with which he won his World Championship in 1958

In 1959 Tony Brooks joined Ferrari. Although he dislikes sports car racing, he drove this 3-litre machine into third place in the 1,000-km. race at the Nürburgring

TONY BROOKS

Racing drivers are seldom type-cast. Bearing out this theory is Tony Brooks, who, without crash helmet and goggles, could hardly look less like a racing driver, who shuns the limelight, and yet is one of the most brilliant of all.

Brooks started racing with one of those excellent, rugged cars, a Healey Silverstone, his first appearance being in March 1952 at Goodwood.

Brooks showed more than the usual amount of talent, graduating to a Le Mans Replica Frazer-Nash in 1953. The following year he was driving for the Frazer-Nash works team when his capabilities were noted by John Wyer, then racing manager of Aston Martin. Tony joined the Feltham-based team in 1955 for four happy, successful seasons.

Perhaps his greatest performance during that time was his victory (with Noel Cunning-ham-Reid) in the Nürburgring 1,000 Kilometres of 1957. And never forget that Brooks made history in October 1955 by winning the Syracuse Grand Prix in a Connaught, the first British driver of a British-built car to win a Grand Prix after the war.

Brooks went to BRM in 1956 for an unhappy year of mechanical breakdowns. Two successful seasons followed with Vanwall, in which he helped the marque win the World Constructors' Championship. This year he has gone to Ferrari where he brought the Italian team its first great victory of the season by winning the Grand Prix of Europe at Rheims in July.

Tony Brooks, a qualified dental surgeon, races for the love of the game, has definite ideas about it. He is a quiet, retiring star who, when on form with a car that responds to his masterly touch, is virtually unbeatable.

HARRY SCHELL

Ebullient, effervescent, sometimes explosive, Harry O'Reilly Schell has been bustin' out all over the racing circuits of Europe and farther afield for so long now that a season without him is unthinkable. He is part of the motor-racing scene and embraces part of its character in his own. To Harry, motor racing is above all, fun. A sport that has its serious side, but one not to get too serious about.

morning, Harry had some difficulty explaining its presence to a poker-faced management who refused to see the joke.

There are few cars that Harry Schell has not driven during his career, Maserati, Ferrari, Vanwall and, currently, BRM. But whatever car he is given, the customers can always be certain that they will get their moneysworth, for Harry will always 'have a go'. On his day, there are few as fast and even fewer faster. No one there will ever forget his

Schell with the BRM rounding the Thillois hairpin at Rheims

Harry Schell is a Franco-American peppered with a dash of Irish from his mother's side of the family. Like all characters, he is slightly larger than life—and sometimes gets himself involved in slightly outrageous goings-on.

Take the night before the 1958 French Grand Prix when a midnight gang, headed by Stirling Moss and Luigi Musso, took Schell's Vespa minicar from the road outside Rheims's Lion D'Or Hotel and left it upstairs in the residents' lounge on the first floor. Next

epic drive in the 1956 French Grand Prix when he lifted the Vanwall from seventh to second place in the few laps before it broke down, thus doing more than anyone else to revive a flagging enthusiasm for the British car.

Recently, Harry's fortunes with the BRM have not rewarded him properly for the effort he has put into driving the car. No one more richly deserves at least one good, thumping win in the car he has stuck to and driven through thick and thin for so long.

JACK BRABHAM

More than one Australian has crossed the world to make his home in Britain, and subsequently to make his name in European motor racing. But all their reputations are currently being overshadowed by a young man called Jack Brabham who, as we write, has won two *grande épreuves* and leads the World Championship in only his fifth season of racing on this side of the globe.

Now aged thirty-three, Brabham has been brought up in a hard school of competitive motoring. Soon after being discharged from the R.A.F. as a Flight Engineer in 1946, Brabham met up with one Johnny Schonberg, an ex-midget car-racing champion from the United States, who came to live round the corner from Jack in Sydney, New South Wales. Schonberg it was who introduced Brabham to midget cars which the latter began driving in 1947 and soon won just about every championship in Australia for racing and hill-climbing them. Later he con-

tinued to mop up championships between 1953 and 1955, firstly with a Cooper Mk. 4 and then a Cooper-Bristol.

In 1955, however, Brabham decided to visit Britain for six months and have a quick look at the European motor-racing scene. He liked it so much he has been here ever since. After a couple of seasons with various cars, he joined the Cooper stable based at Surbiton in 1957—and is with them still.

At first, Brabham's brash cornering technique, a hangover from midget-car days, caused a few raised eyebrows. But soon the young Australian was winning races, and that was what counted. Apart from two or three outings with the Aston Martin team, he has stuck to Coopers ever since. Now, still maintaining and tuning the cars he drives as far as possible, Brabham has it within his power to win the World Championship for Cooper and take the title to the Commonwealth for the first time in history.

Crouching as low as possible in his Cooper to minimize the little car's frontal area, Jack Brabham tears round the circuit in the 1959 Dutch Grand Prix

3 *The 'Big Ten' Cars*

Vanwall

IN 1949, G. A. Vandervell, wealthy manufacturer of almost all the engine bearings used by the British motor industry, bought himself a Ferrari. It was a 1½-litre supercharged car of the type which was being raced that year

G. A. Vandervell

by the Ferrari team itself. Mr. Vandervell had the words 'Thin Wall Special' painted in the car's bonnet and set about running it at Silverstone, where it was driven by Raymond Mays. At that same time, Vandervell was also strongly supporting Mays' original BRM project.

The following year Vandervell returned to Ferrari and purchased one of their latest products, an unsupercharged 4½-litre car. This he also named 'Thin Wall Special'. Between 1950 and 1954 the gigantic 'Thin Wall Special' appeared frequently in Britain and occasionally on the Continent. It was driven by a variety of top-line pilots, amongst them Taruffi, Parnell, Collins and Farina, who used it to score Silverstone's first 100 m.p.h. lap. The car was frequently modified bodily and mechanically and was being used as a mobile research shop with which to gain experience of Grand Prix engineering.

In May of 1954, a new machine made its first appearance, driven by Alan Brown, in the pouring rain at Silverstone. It bore the name 'Vanwall Special'.

In 1955 Britain's hopes for a real Grand Prix winner in the Vanwall were dashed slightly. The car appeared in many races driven by Hawthorn, Ken Wharton and Harry Schell, but on all the important occasions something went wrong mechanically. For 1956 Colin Chapman, of Lotus fame, was

Tony Brooks driving the 1958 Vanwall to win the Italian Grand Prix

called in to redesign the chassis, and his colleague Mike Costin, to provide an aerodynamic body of teardrop shape. With Moss winning at Silverstone and Schell giving convincing high-speed demonstrations at Rheims and Monza, it was obvious by the end of the season that Vandervell really had a potential winner on his hands.

The truth of this was proved in 1957 when Moss and Brooks between them turned a page in motor racing history by being the first British drivers to win a classic Grand Prix in a British car for more than thirty years. And at the end of the season, Moss and the Vanwall also won a fantastic Italian Grand Prix at Monza. Then in 1958 the Vanwalls won six out of ten classic Grand Prix and brought the Constructors' Championship to Britain. Our debt to 'Tony' Vandervell is great indeed.

'Thirty-three seconds ahead of Hawthorn with six laps to go'—the Vanwall team signal Tony Brooks leading the 1958 Grand Prix of Europe at Spa. Extreme left: Team Manager David Yorke. Centre right: Stirling Moss, whose car has retired

Ferrari

Which person has had the greatest single influence on Grand Prix motor racing since the war? There is no doubt about the answer to that question—the Italian Enzo Ferrari.

The story of Enzo Ferrari and motor racing reaches back over thirty years to the days of the 1920's when *Il Commendatore* was himself a well-known racing driver. In the early 1930's, Ferrari retired from the cockpit and founded his own team, the Scuderia Ferrari to race Alfa Romeos. Then in 1933 the Alfa Romeo factory decided to let Ferrari race their official works *monoposto* cars. With the successes that followed, the name of Ferrari was seldom out of the headlines for a couple of seasons. But 1934 saw Nazi Germany enter the Grand Prix field, using it as a means of national publicity. The Nazis threw everything they had into building the invincible Mercedes-Benz and Auto Union teams, which swept all before them right up to the war in 1939.

Between 1946 and 1948 Ferrari returned to the racing game with sports cars, while Alfa Romeo mopped up all the Grand Prix honours. But September 1948 saw the first appearance, in the Italian Grand Prix at Turin, of the Formula 1 Ferrari, a supercharged $1\frac{1}{2}$-litre machine with a V12 engine and well over 200 b.h.p. These cars entered the fray of the European season the following year.

Enzo Ferrari

In addition, one was acquired in Britain and raced by the well-known 'gentleman' driver, Peter Whitehead, another going to Mr. G. A. Vandervell, being raced under the name of 'Thin Wall Special'—and that, as we have seen, was the beginning of the Vanwall story.

For another two years Alfa Romeo continued to reign supreme. But Ferrari finally broke their grip in the British Grand Prix of 1951, when the 'Pampas Bull', Froilan

Jean Behra in the 1959 Ferrari at Aintree.

Dented Ferrari is Phil Hill's—in the Monaco Grand Prix 1959

Gonzalez, put his big unsupercharged 4½-litre car first past the flag after a magnificent drive. Then, by winning the World Championship twice in succession (1952 and 1953) on Ferarri, Alberto Ascari put the cars from Maranello to the top of the tree.

Ferarri was eclipsed by Mercedes-Benz and Fangio in 1954 and 1955, triumphed again (with considerable help from Lancia and Fangio) in 1956, went down to Maserati and Fangio in the following year, and shared the World Championship limelight with Mike Hawthorn's Drivers' win and Vanwall's Constructors' win in 1958. And what a line up of drivers they have had through the years—Farina, Taruffi, Gonzalez, Hawthorn, Villoresi, Ascari, Castellotti, Fangio, Parnell, Musso, Collins and now Brooks and Phil Hill—the list is almost endless.

Team manager Tavoni

Phil Hill
(U.S.A.)

Innes Ireland
(Great Britain)

Graham Hill
(Great Britain)

Joakim Bonnier
(Sweden)

Cliff Allison
(Great Britain)

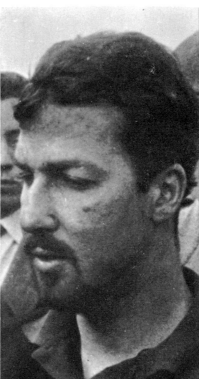

Maserati

In the 1920's, a certain Alfieri Maserati, one of six brothers, ran a small factory which produced sparking plugs at Bologna, in northern Italy. Alfieri's great love was motor racing and in his early days he drove an Italian car called a Diatto with a certain amount of success.

Eventually, like so many owner-drivers, young Alfieri modified his car to such an extent that it was rather more Maserati than Diatto. So he took the logical step and called it by his own name.

Throughout the 1920's and 1930's, the Maserati reputation increased, and the marque's Trident radiator badge was seen everywhere that racing cars foregathered. Successes came and went. Some years were good, others bad, but hardly a race passed without a Maserati entry.

Driven by the 'greats' of the day, amongst them the legendary Nuvolari, the Maseratis stayed in the picture right up to the outbreak of the war.

No sooner was the war over than Maserati,

Omer Orsi

who had moved from Bologna to their present home at Modena in 1937, were back

'*A space-frame car with hardly any space for the space' is how the complicated construction of Maserati's 1959 sports car was described by one magazine*

Maserati engineer and designer, Guilio Alfieri

Guglielmo Dei, director of the Scud Centro-Sud and the Centro-Sud racing driv school, in one of the team's Maseratis at Modena HQ

in motor racing once again. In 1946 they fielded two new 1½-litre supercharged cars which almost certainly must have been planned and built at Modena while the war was still going strong. One of these, the 4CL was developed into the tubular-chassied 4CLT, and later into famous 'San Remo' Maserati, two of the most attractive racing cars ever bult.

In 1947 the two remaining Maserati brothers sold their factory, their racing cars and their Trident badge to the Orsis, Adolfo and his son Omer, who now run them as part of the huge Orsi industrial enterprise which even includes the somewhat archaic Sicilian railways! Incidentally, it is not generally appreciated that the principal product of the Modena works nowadays is machine tools of the very highest quality. And how incongruous they look, too, lined up alongside the sleek, expensive high-performance cars built in the same factory.

At Rouen in July, the new 2-litre sports Maserati made its first appearance.
With Stirling Moss at the wheel it scored an impressive victory.

In it up to the ears (and beyond). A Cooper mechanic tending his charge before a race

Swedish driver Joakim Bonnier with the BRM. This combination won the Dutch Grand Prix of 1959, BRM's first World Championship victory after ten years of effort

B.R.M.

The BRM story started immediately after the war, when Raymond Mays and Peter Berthon set about the task of building a racing car which would put Britain right on the Grand Prix map, as the Mercedes-Benz and Auto Unions had done for Germany during the 1930's. Mays and Berthon had previously been responsible for the design and development of the very successful (and relatively simple) series of E.R.A. racing cars. Now Berthon embarked on a design for a $1\frac{1}{2}$-litre supercharged car with 16 cylinders. In every respect, its design was 'very advanced', to say the least.

The V16 car was first demonstrated to the Press in December 1949. It failed to leave the grid in its first race, the British Grand

Alfred Owen, chief of the Owen Organization and the BRM project

50

Prix, the following summer and, one way and another, failed to make any real impression on motor racing during the next five years. That the BRM was fantastically fast was undeniable—and fantastically impressive in the ear-splitting noises it made too. Unfortunately its specification seemed to be too advanced for the resources available.

In 1953 the whole BRM project was taken over by the engineering group of Rubery, Owen & Co. Ltd., whose millionaire chief, Alfred Owen, had been one of the original backers of the car. And with the 2½-litre Formula 1 coming into force in 1954, Berthon went ahead to design a new 4-cylinder BRM.

This car was a far simpler design than its predecessor, but regrettably it must be admitted that it suffered from just as many troubles, even under private ownership. Right through 1956, 1957 and 1958 the BRM appeared in nearly every major Grand Prix in the calendar. But, although it frequently showed a remarkable turn of speed, something always went wrong. Parts of the engine broke, the roadholding went seriously astray

Team chief Raymond Mays discusses BRM technicalities with the car's designer Peter Berthon (right)

and the brakes either failed to work at all, or worked too well and seized solid.

Then, during the winter of 1958–59, the car was given a major mechanical 'facelift' with highly satisfactory results. For at the end of May 1959, the Swedish driver Joakim Bonnier climbed into the BRM at Zandvoort and triumphantly won the Dutch Grand Prix. It was the end of a long, hard road.

Mainstay and chief test driver of the BRM team for many years has been Scotsman Ron Flockhart, seen here at Monaco.

Texan racing driver Carroll Shelby with the 1959 Grand Prix Aston Martin at Silverstone

Aston Martin

Before we go any further, let us settle the matter of the name. No, it was not a case of a Mr. Aston meeting a Mr. Martin and deciding to build cars. It was a case of a Mr. Martin building cars after the 1914–18 war and driving them successfully at a well-known hillclimb near London—the Aston Clinton hillclimb to be precise.

Lionel Martin and Robert Bamford built their first car in 1913. But after the war

Bamford retired and Martin took over their business completely with financial help from that amazing (to put it mildly) character, Count Louis Zborowski. From the very start in 1921 Lionel Martin built sports and touring cars which quickly gained a unique reputation for performance coupled with reliability, both on the roads and in competitions of all kinds.

In 1927 Aston Marton Limited was taken over by A. C. Bertelli, a well-known racing driver, and it changed hands yet again in 1932. But throughout the years up to the 1939–45 war, the reputation of the company's products went from strength to strength.

Shortly after the world settled down again to enjoy what it called peace, Aston Martin found itself under new ownership once more. This time it had been -taken over by the industrialist David Brown, who carried on the sporting tradition of Aston Martin.

On the racing front, Aston Martin re-entered the international fray in earnest in 1950 and have been there ever since. Starting with the DB2 gaining honours at Le Mans in their first year, their sporting achievements

David Brown (left) with the well-known French motoring journalist Bernard Cahier

1959 newcomer—the Formula I Aston Martin during practice for the Dutch Grand Prix. At the wheel; Carroll Shelby

Monaco Grand Prix 1959. Above: *French champion Maurice Trintignant with Rob Walker's Cooper-Clim*
Below: *Tony Brooks driving the short-nosed Formula I Ferrari*

have been far too numerous to quote here in any detail.

The first David Brown Aston Martin to be designed specifically for racing was the DB3S, and this model finished second at Le Mans on three occasions, 1955, 1956 and 1958. It also won the Tourist Trophy in 1953, and all three Goodwood 9-Hour Races. But perhaps the marque's greatest achievement to date has been victory three years in succession, for the current DBR1/300 model, in the exhausting, seven-hour-long, 1,000 Kilometres of the Nürburgring.

And now 1959 has seen the debut of the Aston Martin Grand Prix car, a further big step in keeping with the marque's traditions. That, and the magnificent win at their tenth attempt of the 24 Hours at Le Mans—a truly outstanding performance.

Moss and Fairman with the winners' laurels after winning the Nürburgring 1000-km. race in an Aston Martin

Stirling Moss on the limit with the 3-litre Aston Martin DBR1/300 at Silverstone, 1958

Cooper

Charles Cooper's father intended that his son should follow the family tradition and go on the stage. But young Charles had different ideas from a very early age. Far from being interested in things theatrical, his only love was for things mechanical. Even in his school-days Charles's mind was engaged with unusual, but intriguing technical exercises.

Fortunately, Charles Cooper's obvious talents were soon channelled into more conventional lines. Before long he was in the car business with his own garage in London, and up to the ears in motor racing and flying. And before long, he, too, was the father of a son, John Newton Cooper. It was to be cars or nothing for young John.

But, to skip forward some years. In 1946, dismayed by the expense involved in going motor racing, John Cooper decided to build

John Cooper (left) *with his No. 1 team driver, the Australian Jack Brabham*

himself a small, cheap car, also using a motorcycle engine for its source of power. This machine, the Cooper 500, was so successful after development that, in 1948, a certain

Charles Cooper

wavy-haired young man in his teens bought one with which to start his racing career. The young man's name was Stirling Moss.

In the years that followed, Moss made his name in half-litre racing, while Cooper almost literally 'made' half-litre racing. Apart from some opposition from Kieft, Cooper cars dominated the 500 c.c. scene. Then, looking

R.R.C. (Rob) Walker, for whose team of privately-owned Coopers, prepared by tuning wizard Alf Francis, Stirling Moss has won several major victories

Jack Brabham in the 2½-litre 'works' Cooper-Climax on his way to winning the Monaco Grand Prix 1959

for fresh fields to conquer, the Coopers designed the Formula 2 2-litre Cooper-Bristol.

The Cooper-Bristol motored extremely quickly, especially in Hawthorn's hands, but it was never a match for the Italian works cars in major Grands Prix. The engine just could not produce enough steam. Then, in 1955, there appeared the first of a new line of Coopers. This was an aerodynamically-shaped sports car powered by the 1,100 c.c. Coventry-Climax engine.

From that time right up to the present day,

it has been Coventry-Climax all the way for Coopers. The cars have developed in step with the engine, and vice versa. Both the sports cars and those for the current Formula 2 have distinguished themselves in races all over the world, often against seemingly over-powering opposition. Moss and Trintignant have won Formula 1 Grands Prix in them. And now, with the latest full 2½-litre engine, Jack Brabham gave the works team its first World Championship victory at Monaco last May.

Private owner Jim Russell driving his Climax-engined sports Cooper Monaco

Ferry Porsche (right) *with racing manager Huschke von Hanstein*

Porsche

Not many engineers can claim to have designed both a world-beating racing car and a world-beating economy passenger car. The problems inherent in each design are so totally divorced that the man who can tackle one successfully generally leaves the other strictly alone.

But one who had sufficient skill for both jobs was the German engineer, Ferdinand Porsche. Before the war he was responsible for the series of amazing, rear-engined Auto Union racing cars which, in company with the Mercedes-Benz cars, all but wiped the floor with every other marque in Europe. And he was also responsible for the design of the extraordinary 'People's Car', the Volkswagen, a vehicle which was conceived as long ago as 1931 and which is still selling in its thousands, basically unaltered, nearly thirty years later.

The racing Porsches we see on the circuits today are direct descendants of the Volkswagens. When all the expensive, performance-gaining trimmings have been taken away from the engine, the 'bed rock' of the design is Volkswagen through and through.

The first Porsche, with its flat-four, air-cooled 'engine in the boot', appeared in 1949. The car found a ready market, which has increased steadily ever since. Now offered in 1,500 c.c. and 1,600 c.c. form, production has increased but has never caught up with demand. And it is a firm endorsement of Ferdinand Porsche's original design that, although many minor modifications have been made, the car has never been altered basically during its ten years of existence.

As for the stark, rectangular racing Porsches which mop up major awards year after year —the most amazing thing about them is where on earth their fantastic speed comes from. They still have their little 'flat four' engines, but each season they go faster and faster, never apparently reaching an ultimate limit, or even being in sight of one. The secret is, of course, steady development coupled with immaculate preparation.

Making its first appearance at Monaco in 1959, with Wolfgang von Trips at the wheel, was the Grand Prix Porsche for the 1961 Formula

H.R.H. the Duke of Kent is a keen motor racing and photography enthusiast, and on the Continent he can often avoid protocol and go to the races simply as one of the crowd. Here, at Zandvoort, he joins anonymously a trio of press photographers to take a picture of one of the drivers in the 1959 Dutch Grand Prix

Tony Brooks and Stirling Moss—footwear view

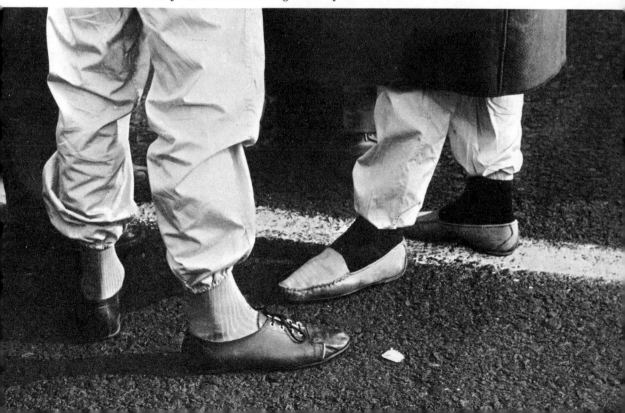

The sports Porsche Spyder RSK, driven at Nürburgring by the Belgian motoring journalist and Grand Prix pilot, Paul Frere

However, with four overhead camshafts and two plugs per cylinder, this development has now reached the stage where a label might almost be attached to the racing engine reading, 'Any similarity between this unit and a Volkswagen engine is purely coincidental!'

Not content with remaining in the sports car field, Ferry Porsche, Ferdinand's son, who took over the firm on his father's death in 1951, and his racing manager, Huschke von Hanstein, this year produced a new machine. This was a prototype Grand Prix car designed for the new Formula 1 which comes into force in 1961.

Airfield race at Zeltweg in 1958. Wolfgang von Trips, in front of Jean Behra, leads the Porsche works team

Graham Hill at the wheel of the sports Lotus Seventeen with Coventry-Climax engine

Lotus

Still with only ten years behind him as a designer of motor cars, Anthony Colin Bruce Chapman has already been hailed as a genius of automobile engineering.

Colin Chapman built his first car in 1948. It was a trials special with a 1930 Austin Seven saloon basis, and it was christened 'Lotus'. This was followed by a second Lotus, incorporating many improvements and with a 1,172 c.c. Ford engine. Most of this machine was thought out while Chapman was in the R.A.F., and put together during leaves and week-ends. After he was demobilized, Colin set about a full competition season of trials and speed events throughout 1950.

The following year brought the 750 c.c. Austin-engined racing Mk. 3 Lotus, and with 1953 came the Mks. 4 and 5 trials cars.

By this time Chapman and his helpers had become the Lotus Engineering Company, and their next car, the Mk. 6, really put them on the map, despite the fact that the company almost went bankrupt within months of its formation! Engines of various kinds were used in the racing Mk. 6, which was built in some quantity for sale to private

Colin Chapman

Motor racing the cheap way

How they clear the track in France (The Gendarme 'broom')

The 2½-litre Coventry-Climax Formula 1 Lotus, driven by Graham Hill

owner-drivers. Some had M.G. units, others Ford Consul, but most were equipped with the 1,172 c.c. Ford engine, and with this the car was virtually unbeatable in its class for two years. Later came the 1,100 c.c. Coventry-Climax 'fire pump' engine, and this, together with the arrival of one Mike Costin, changed the Lotus fortunes.

For besides Mike's considerable talents came those of his brother, Frank, who was then an aerodynamicist with De Havilland. Together the team gave sports racing cars an entirely new shape, long, low and sleek, and an entirely new degree of performance. Since then, each year has seen at least one new model Lotus and their successes on the circuits of the world must run into hundreds.

From sports cars, Colin Chapman progressed to designing out-and-out Formula racing cars, first

Formula 2, then Formula 1 Grand Prix machines. He was also called in by both BRM and Vanwall, who realized that his incredible facility for solving road-holding problems could solve problems on their cars that they had been puzzling over for months.

But one enigma concerning Colin Chapman remains—why did he give his first car the name 'Lotus'? The question still remains unanswered—even after ten years.

Parts of the Lotus which are literally 'tied together with elastic bands' are the fuel and oil tanks of the Formula 1 car !

Ivor Bueb driving an Ecurie Ecosse Jaguar D through the Esses at Le Mans

Jaguar

Jaguar Cars Limited stemmed from very small beginnings in Blackpool, Lancashire, in 1922, where a young man called Bill Lyons opened a small side-street workshop and put up a signboard which read: The Swallow Sidecar and Coachbuilding Company. Before long Lyons' business had expanded and was building special bodywork for de luxe versions of various small cars. There was the Austin-Swallow, the Standard-Swallow and the Swift-Swallow.

From this Lyons progressed to building cars of his own after taking over an old factory in Coventry. At first these vehicles were based on Standard chassis and engines. Later Lyons engaged a young engineer called William Heynes to design an engine, and the first car to bear the Jaguar name appeared in 1935.

After the war, Lyons (soon to become Sir William) attacked export markets with the sensational Jaguar XK 120, with its Heynes-designed six-cylinder engine. This low-priced car completely altered the whole conception of sports car motoring, and from it stemmed the C-type and D-type line of sports-racing cars which swept into the world's headlines with their first-time-out at Le Mans victory in 1951. They won again as a works team in 1953 and 1955. And in both 1956 and 1957 it was the privately-owned Scottish stable, Ecurie Ecosse, run by David Murray, which fielded the D-types that scored Jaguar's fourth and fifth triumphs in the gruelling Grand Prix d'Endurance.

Jaguar boss Sir William Lyons with his chief engineer William Heynes (left) designer of the world-famous XK engine

Lister-Jaguar

In a quiet backwater of the university town of Cambridge you will find the small, rather old-fashioned workshops of George Lister and Sons Limited, constructional engineers and architectural metal workers. One of the sons of one of the sons in the firm's title, is Brian Lister, the energetic force behind the very fast Lister-Jaguar sports cars which appear frequently on the racing circuits of Europe.

After spending the war in the R.A.F., Brian Lister returned to Cambridge with an interest in cars. He modified and raced various different models including M.G., Morgan and Cooper-M.G. Then, in 1953, he decided to build a car to his own design. The result was a Lister-M.G., to be followed by a Lister-Bristol, which scored many successes in the hands of that great little driver Archie Scott-Brown.

Later there followed the Jaguar-engined Lister, a big car with a big performance which, teamed with Archie, made an almost unbeatable combination.

However, after Le Mans this year Brian Lister retired from active participation in motor racing. It is to be hoped that this move is only temporary.

Brian Lister

Bruce Halford's Lister-Jaguar leads the first-lap queue in a sports-car race at Crystal Palace

In the hush of a May calm, Donald Campbell sculls gently out on the glassy surface of the deep blue lake at Coniston. To check the water. With him goes Woppit, the fastest waterborne bear in the world. Woppit is Campbell's mascot. A good-luck charm that goes everywhere with him.

A perfect reflection. The turbo-jet hydroplane Bluebird flashes across Coniston water

4
astest of All

FEW reputations are harder to keep up than that of being the son of a famous father. And this is particularly true where the son follows precisely in his father's footsteps. Donald Campbell, however, is an excellent example of the exception which proves the rule.

During the nineteen-twenties and nineteen-thirties, Sir Malcolm Campbell's exploits in breaking the world's land and water speed records with his boats and cars named 'Bluebird' became part of the history of British achievement in automobile and nautical engineering.

However, the existing 'fastest on earth' record is credited to John Cobb's Railton Special in 1947 at 394·20 m.p.h. But now Donald Campbell believes it is high time that the record was raised once more—and that

Donald Campbell with his wife and Leo Villa after breaking the World Water Speed record at Coniston in May 1959

it should be reclaimed by the Campbell family.

During the past few years, Donald, his Chief Mechanic Leo Villa and their enthusiastic team have devoted unlimited time and energy to the problem of reaching unprecedented speeds on water. With the aid of the latest turbo-jet propelled hydroplane 'Bluebird' they achieved a fantastic 260·35 m.p.h. on Coniston Water last May. In future runs they hope to do even better, and a round 300 m.p.h. is their final aim.

But the next target is the land speed record. And in this direction, 1960 will see the trials of Campbell's new 4,000 h.p. turbo-jet car which is at present being built by the same firm who were responsible for the construction of 'Bluebird'. The speed aimed for is no less than 475 m.p.h. and then, eventually, 500 m.p.h.

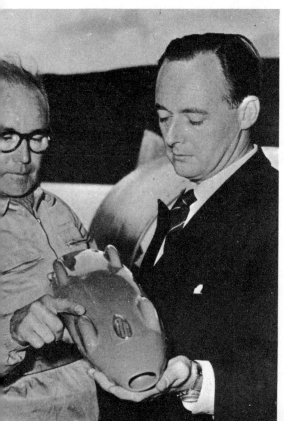

Donald Campbell and Leo Villa with the model of the turbo-jet car Bluebird for the proposed attempt on the World's Land Speed record

5 Some Leading Circuits

The wide open spaces of Silverstone. Leading past the pits are Peter Collins (Ferrari), Stirling Moss (Vanwall) and Mike Hawthorn (Ferrari) in the British Grand Prix, 1958

Silverstone

BRITAIN has never allowed her public roads to be used for motor racing. Consequently, circuits have had to be found on private property. Once we had Brooklands and Donington Park. After the war when Britain had to find a new circuit, it dawned on someone that the perimeter track of some of the aerodromes deserted by the R.A.F. would make racing tracks. So the R.A.C. approached the Air Ministry.

Then, so the story goes, someone in the Government told the Ministry that if they intended letting out a piece of their property for this nasty, dirty, noisy sport, it had better be tucked well out of the way. Thus Silverstone, an ex-bomber airfield in one of the remoter parts of Northamptonshire, came into the hands of the R.A.C.

Silverstone was first raced on in October 1948. And from 1949 onwards it became the home of the British Grand Prix. Nowadays the Grand Prix alternates between Silverstone and Aintree, but the circuit is still well used. Countless club race meetings are held there—virtually one a week for six months of the year.

Being an airfield, Silverstone differs from every other Grand Prix circuit. Its track is wide, but virtually flat and featureless. The corners look tight, but can be taken very quickly indeed by drivers with the right amount of dash. This is obvious from the lap record, which stands at well over 100 m.p.h.

Lap Distance: 2·93 miles.

Location: 5 miles west of Towcester, Northamptonshire.

Lap Record: Jean Behra (2½-litre BRM) and Peter Collins (2½-litre Ferrari), 1 min. 40 sec., 105·37 m.p.h. during the *Daily Express* International Trophy Race, May 1958. Equalled by Roy Salvadori (2½-litre Aston Martin) during the Trophy Meeting, May 1959.

Goodwood

Now the home of Britain's classic race, the Tourist Trophy for sports cars, Goodwood started life as an R.A.F. airfield. During the war it was Westhampnett fighter base, one of the famous Battle of Britain airfields which included Tangmere.

In 1946, a well-known racing driver, the Australian Tony Gaze, who had been stationed at Westhampnett, suggested that the perimeter track would make a good racing circuit. The Duke of Richmond and Gordon, on whose Goodwood Estate the airfield lay, thought so too. The result—two years later, in September 1948, the new track saw its first race meeting.

Goodwood is used for racing exclusively by the British Automobile Racing Club, the post-war descendant of the Brooklands Automobile Racing Club. And it has virtually taken the place of Brooklands as both a speed and social centre. On a fine summer's day, this circuit in the lee of the Sussex Downs is as attractive as any, and at a big meeting the paddock has quite a garden party air about it.

With its succession of right-hand bends,

Goodwood is a fast circuit. However, as it is mainly used by sports cars, it has taken some time for a 100 m.p.h. lap to be recorded. This was achieved, unofficially though, by Stirling Moss on a trial run with a BRM in April 1959. Moss, incidentally, made his first big appearance at Goodwood in the 1948 opening meeting, winning the half-litre race in his first car, a Cooper.

Lap Distance: 2·4 miles.

Location: 2 miles north of Chichester, Sussex.

Lap Record: Mike Hawthorn (2½-litre Ferrari) and Stirling Moss (1½-litre Cooper-Climax), 1 min. 28·8 sec., 97·30 m.p.h., at the Easter Monday meeting, April 1958.

Aintree

The Aintree circuit came into being in May 1954. Built by Mrs. Mirabel Topham immediately outside her famous Grand National racecourse, and running parallel to it for much of the distance, Aintree has features similiar to both road and airfield circuits, and one in particular lamentably lacking at nearly every other British circuit. It has a vast permanent grandstand where one can watch the racing and have a snack or a drink on a wet day without having to get soaked or walk through inches of mud.

Aintree's short career has already seen two events of the utmost importance in British motor racing. It was here that Stirling Moss won the British Grand Prix in 1955, and where he also became the first British driver to win a *Grande Épreuve* in a British car for thirty-five years. This was in 1957, when Moss and Tony Brooks drove a Vanwall over the line first in the European Grand Prix.

From the driver's point of view, Aintree is not as simple a circuit as it might at first appear. True, there are two good straights and a couple of fast bends, but the infield Country Loop contains corners which call for fine judgement and a lot of gearbox work.

The result of overdoing the chicane at Goodwood. Mike Hawthorn's Ferrari passes Jean Behra's bent BRM

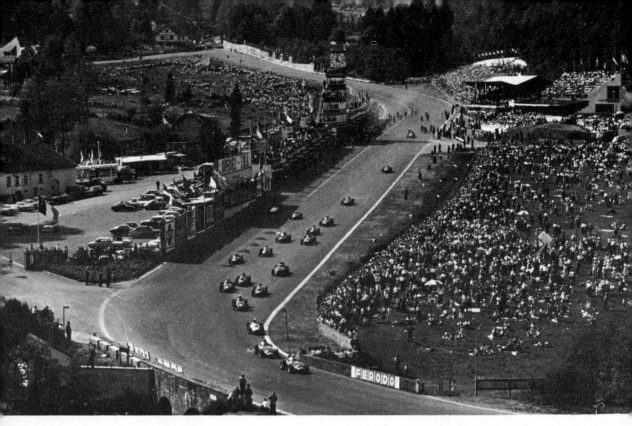

Scenic grandeur of the Spa circuit, Belgium. This is the start of the 1958 Grand Prix

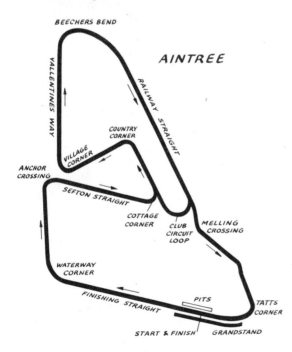

AINTREE

BEECHERS BEND
VALLENTINES WAY
RAILWAY STRAIGHT
COUNTRY CORNER
VILLAGE CORNER
ANCHOR CROSSING
SEFTON STRAIGHT
COTTAGE CORNER
CLUB CIRCUIT LOOP
MELLING CROSSING
WATERWAY CORNER
FINISHING STRAIGHT
PITS
TATTS CORNER
START & FINISH
GRANDSTAND

Whether this northern circuit or Silverstone is the best venue for the British Grand Prix is a hotly contested matter of opinion, to which there can probably never be a definite answer.

Lap Distance: 3 miles.

Location: 5 miles north of the centre of Liverpool.

Lap Record: Stirling Moss ($2\frac{1}{2}$-litre BRM) and Bruce McLaren ($2\frac{1}{2}$-litre Cooper -Climax), 1 min. 57·0 sec., 92·31 m.p.h. during the British Grand Prix, July 1959.

Oulton Park

If the holding of Championship races on them is to be the yardstick by which circuits are included or excluded from this book, then Oulton Park has no right to be here. Nor for that matter has Brands Hatch. But both venues are slightly special, and for that reason they appear.

The excellent Oulton Park track has as

Right: *With the mountains of Sicily in the background, Jean Behra's Porsche passes a roadside café during the 1958 Targa Florio*

many of the attributes of the true road circuit as are ever likely to be found on private property. Set in the parkland of an estate not far from Chester, it winds in and out and up and down through trees, and beside a lake straight into which more than one driver has been known to go, complete with car!

Oulton Park, similar in many ways to pre-war Donington, is no easy circuit for the driver. It demands an entirely different approach from Silverstone, Goodwood or Aintree, if only from the point of view of there being absolutely no room for over-enthusiasm. Running out of road here means unpleasant consequences, not just a spin on wide open spaces. But every competent driver likes, or at the very least respects, the circuit, seeing in it a far greater challenge to driving skill than exists on an airfield.

As for the spectators, the circuit could hardly be more attractive. They are not tied to any particular spot and can wander from corner to corner, picnicking beneath the trees and enjoying an atmosphere unique in British motor racing today.

Lap Distance: 2·76 miles.

Location: Near Tarporley, Cheshire. 10 miles south of Chester.

Lap Record: Stirling Moss (3-litre Aston Martin) and Graham Hill (1½-litre Lotus), 1 min. 50·8 sec., 89·70 m.p.h., during the British Empire Trophy race, April 1958.

Brands Hatch

Brands Hatch, the circuit on London's doorstep, has a far longer history than most people imagine. It has, in fact, been in use since 1928, though before the war it was a simple grass-track for motor cycle events. Not until 1950 did it become a proper tar-mac circuit for motor cars, at which time it was the cradle of 500 c.c. racing.

The half-litre cars and Brands Hatch were ideally suited to one another, the mile-long kidney-shaped circuit because it lay in a natural amphitheatre from the sides of which the track could be seen all the way round. Moreover, the length and width of the circuit did not dwarf the little Coopers and Kiefts, as sometimes happened at Silverstone and Goodwood.

In 1954 the Druids Hill loop was added. It only increased the lap distance by a quarter of a mile, but introduced an interesting semi-hairpin and a downhill dash with an extremely tricky bend at the bottom.

In recent years the general popularity of half-litre racing has waned in the face of opposition from sports cars. Events for these machines now form the staple diet at Brands Hatch. Formula 1 racing has been tried, but the circuit is just not long enough for the bigger cars to get 'wound up'. However, another extension is planned to make every kind of race possible, at which time the already ever-increasing popularity of Brands Hatch is certain to leap still further ahead.

Lap Distance: 1·24 miles.

Location: On the main London–Maidstone road (A20). Two miles south of Farningham, Kent; 15 miles from London.

Lap Record: Jack Brabham (1½-litre Cooper-Climax) and Graham Hill (1½-litre Lotus), 56·6 sec., 78·87 m.p.h., during the International Meeting, August 1959.

Rheims

The triangular, bullet-fast road circuit of Rheims, outside the champagne capital of France, is the scene of the traditional Grand Prix of the Automobile Club of France.

To many the French Grand Prix is the highspot of the year, and certainly during race week the whole town bubbles over with an effervescent gaiety matching that of the local wine. The mid-summer weather of northern France is hot, sometimes overpowering-ly so. Out at the circuit the bright colours shimmer in the sun. It's shirt-sleeves and gay cotton frocks for everyone in the bustling

Left: *Retired maestro Juan Manuel Fangio* (centre) *chatting at Monza with Lotus designer Colin Chapman* (left) *and Lotus driver Graham Hill*

Bruce McLaren
(New Zealand)

Roy Salvadori
(Great Britain)

Ivor Bueb
(Great Britain)

Carroll Shelby
(United States)

Masten Gregory
(United States)

Wolfgang von Trips
(Germany)

Maria Theresa de Filippis
(Italy)

Ron Flockhart
(Great Britain)

Maurice Trintignant
(France)

Jim Russell
(Great Britain)

Olivier Gendebien
(Belgium)

crowd and a never-ending stream of music echoes and re-echoes between concrete pits and concrete grandstands.

The bars sell glasses of ice-cold champagne by the thousand, and pretty girls parade through the paddock trying to take their countrymen's minds off motor cars for a moment. Generally they succeed. And, as race time approaches an electric atmosphere of excited anticipation builds up, helped

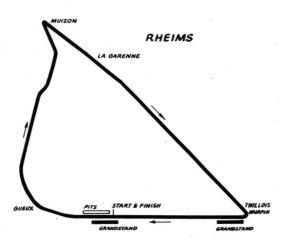

RHEIMS

considerably by the voice on the public address system, which makes every little announcement sound as urgent and important as a royal decree. Yes, the French Grand Prix at Rheims has an air all its own which makes the race a 'must' for many British enthusiasts, who time their summer holidays to coincide with it. If any Continental race is not to be missed, this one ties with Le Mans for the honour.

The circuit itself consists of two long, swooping straights and a mile and a half of flat-out curves, connected by acute corners. It is enormously fast and has seen some of the most dramatic high-speed battles of the last decade. In almost every way Rheims is unique, offering motor racing which is everything that it should be.

Lap Distance: 5·2 miles.
Location: 5 miles north-west of Rheims, on the Soissons Road (N31).
Lap Record: Stirling Moss (2½-litre BRM), 2 min. 22·8 sec., 130·1 m.p.h., during the French Grand Prix, July 1959.

Monaco

Gay, glamorous, tinsel-bright Monte Carlo, where millionaires' yachts tie up in the harbour, where the houses look as though they are built on top of each other. This is the setting for the Grand Prix which opens each European season.

The Monaco Grand Prix is no carefree, high-speed dice. On the contrary, the cars have to grope their way round the two-mile circuit like a reveller getting home after a party. Why? Because this is the 'race of a thousand corners', the original round-the-houses Grand Prix, and now the only one of its kind left in the World Championship.

The circuit winds in and out through the narrow, hilly, twisting streets of Monte Carlo. And on each side are the solid stone walls of hotels, cafés, shops and houses, waiting to catch the over-eager driver careless enough to put a wheel out of place even for the briefest second. The slightest error of judgement here and the result is always a hopping mad team manager and a hefty repair bill.

The start and the pits are on the pavement part of the promenade next to the harbour. The track doubles back on itself, swoops uphill, then left and right in front of the Casino. Then downhill again, through more hairpin bends past the railway station, to the sea-front and a 400-yard tunnel where they use a score of huge spotlights to try to equal the brilliance of the Mediterranean sun outside. Here you need leech-like roadholding, brakes that never lose their grip, a gearbox tough as granite and jet-propelled acceleration. Sheer top speed will get you nowhere.

Flashing round the Monza banking are the Indianapolis cars of Pat O'Connor, Eddie Sachs and Jimmy Bryan

The Monaco Grand Prix circuit at Monte Carlo, where the streets are narrow and the houses look as though they are built on top of each other

Lap Distance: 1·94 miles.
Location: Monte Carlo, Monaco.
Lap Record: Jack Brabham (2½-litre Cooper-Climax), 1 min. 40·4 sec., 70·075 m.p.h., during the Monaco Grand Prix, May 1959.

Monza

In the nineteen twenties, when Brooklands was Britain's home of motor racing, the Italian equivalent was Monza. We have been careless enough to have Brooklands taken from us, but the Italians still have Monza—a bigger and better Monza than ever before.

Built in 1922, this artificial road circuit in a royal park outside Milan has been altered in layout on several occasions, but is, as it has always been, the scene of the Italian Grand Prix. Run in the late summer, in the oppressive heat of the Plain of Lombardy, this event has an air of its own, underlined by

frequent outbursts of Latin temperament.

As it stands now, Monza really consists of two separate layouts. One includes the recently added high-speed track, the other does not, the plan of the whole thing looking, as one writer has said, 'like some super-model railway'.

The oblong *pista di alta velocita*, with its high concrete bankings at both ends, was used for the Grand Prix for the first (and, so far, last) time in 1956. Tremendously high speeds

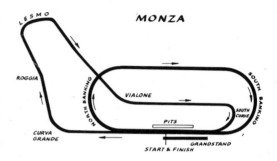

78

were possible, but the bankings turned out to be extremely bumpy.

Thereafter the more normal layout was used once more. This winds through wooded parkland at the Lesmo corners, runs parallel to the finishing straight after Vialone and returns via the South Curve. It is still a very fast circuit with an average speed well over 100 m.p.h., and is, of course, the one on which the Italian teams try hardest to defend their honour—though with singularly little success in the past few years.

Lap Distance: Road circuit, 3·6 miles. High speed circuit, 2·62 miles. Road and high speed circuits combined, 6·2 miles.

Location: 12 miles north-west of Milan, Northern Italy.

Lap Record: Road circuit—Stirling Moss (2½-litre Mercedes-Benz), 2 min. 46·9 sec., 134·0 m.p.h. during the Italian Grand Prix, September 1955.

Nürburgring

Only the Germans could have built the Nürburgring. There is something Teutonically overwhelming about it with its rolling hills clad in deep pine forests and its fairytale castle perched high over the whole scene. This magnificent, fascinating 14-mile succession of twists, turns, swoops and plunges was built through virgin forest in 1927 as part of a plan to help reduce Germany's serious unemployment. Except in 1959 the German Grand Prix has been held there ever since.

Few drivers have ever mastered the Nürburgring, and even then their mastery is tempered with the greatest respect, for the circuit of more than 170 corners is always waiting to catch them unawares. This is the circuit for the true maestro only. Not even the luckiest novice could win here. But the real driver at the peak of his art would trade one Nürburgring for a hundred Silverstones.

From the spectator's point of view, the

setting is beautiful. But the cars only come round every ten minutes or so—only fifteen times in a whole Grand Prix—and it's a long walk from corner to corner. Incidentally, Nürburgring is one of the few racing circuits where the general public can 'have a go' during the year. Pay a shilling or two and you can pit your car's time against a Ferrari's and your skill against Fangio's. People do it all the time—and the track authorities are by now quite philosophic about the over-confident souls who come unstuck!

Lap Distance: 14 miles.

Location: In the Eifel Mountains, 45 miles south of Cologne, 70 miles south-east of Aachen, Western Germany.

Stretching away into the far distance is the long finishing straight of the super-fast Rheims circuit, scene of the French Grand Prix

Spa

Belgium's Grand Prix course, the Francor-champs circuit near Spa, is similar to Nür-burgring in that it is reasonably long, and winds through hilly, wooded country. But there the similarity ends abruptly. For Spa is one of Europe's fastest circuits.

Its eight and three-quarter miles of road run along both sides of a valley in the Ardennes. When it first came into use in the middle of the nineteen-twenties, the road was narrow, rough and slow. But in recent years, continual improvement has smoothed out the surface, and cambered and reduced the bends. The Belgian Grand Prix average speed (Brooks, Vanwall, 1958) is now the highest of any in Europe.

One of the most unusual features of Spa is that the pits are built on a fairly steep downhill slope. After the start, the road winds into the country to the famous Masta straight. This has a notorious kink in the middle. Then follows the corner at Stavelot village, which used to be a hairpin once upon a time, and the dash back along the other side of the valley through the left-hand Blanchi-mont Corner which has claimed the lives of two of our best drivers, Richard Seaman before the war and Archie Scott-Brown in 1958. The lap ends with the hairpin at La Source.

Spa is spectacular for both spectator and driver. For the latter it takes courage to go through all those bends and curves at full throttle. And if there is a motto that should hang over the bed of every Spa driver, it must be 'Keep your foot down!'

Lap Distance: 8·76 miles.

Location: 10 miles east of Spa, 30 miles south-east of Liège, Belgium.

Lap Record: Mike Hawthorn (2½-litre Ferrari), 3 min. 58·3 sec., 132·36 m.p h., during the European Grand Prix, June 1958.

Zandvoort

Odd, but the story of the building of Zandvoort circuit is part of the history of the Nazi wartime occupation of Holland.

Before the war there was no motor racing in Holland, and no circuit. Then, with the enemy, came destruction and the little seaside town of Zandvoort, near Haarlem, did not escape. But when it came to clearing up the ruins to which much of his town had been reduced, the Burgomaster of Zandvoort had an idea. He would use the debris as the basis for a road. Better still, for a road racing circuit which would attract people, and so business, to Zandvoort when all the fighting was over.

Compared with some of the grander circuits of Europe, Zandvoort is not particularly exciting. It has only one feature of any great difficulty—the double bend of the Hunzerug, where the road runs round the back of the pits. However, the circuit has seen some excellent racing, and its friendly, 'go racing for the fun of it' atmosphere contrasts pleasantly with the rather heavy professional-ism of some of the larger circuits.

Lap Distance: 2·6 miles.

Location: On Dutch coast near Haarlem.

Lap Record: Stirling Moss (2½-litre Cooper-Climax), 1 min. 36·7 m.p.h., 96·99 m.p.h., during the Dutch Grand Prix, May 1959.

Casablanca

Before the war when Mussolini ruled much of it, North Africa was a centre of Grand Prix racing and the Grand Prix of Tripoli ranked amongst the Grandes Épreuves. The 1937 event there still qualifies as the fastest road race ever run. After the war the sport returned to North Africa, Casablanca in French Morocco.

Casablanca had had a racing circuit for

many years. It was used from the late 1920s until 1934. But the post-war ambition of the organizers, the Automobile Club of Morocco, was to stage a World Championship race at Casablanca. To take over where Tripoli left off, in fact.

It took them quite a long time and a great deal of hard work. But with tremendous effort and energy, they managed it. The Grand Prix of Morocco was included in the World Championship list for the first time in 1957.

This North African Grande Épreuve is run over the new, four and three-quarter mile Anfa road circuit outside Casablanca. It takes place in the sunlight and warmth of October, at a time when England is settling down to the dismal murkiness of late autumn. The circuit itself is well-surfaced and extremely fast, allowing a race average of well over 100 m.p.h.

Lap Distance: 4·72 miles.

Location: Casablanca, French Morocco, North Africa.

Lap Record: Stirling Moss (2½-litre Vanwall), 2 min. 22·5 sec., 117·86 m.p.h., during the Moroccan Grand Prix, October 1958.

Le Mans

It is one minute to four on a Saturday afternoon in mid-June.

'One minute more and then we shall see, all fifty-four of us, what the weeks of preparation have brought. All eyes turn towards the starter. Then suddenly it is four o'clock. And the patter of fifty-four pairs of feet is heard quite plainly as they race across the track. Another moment's silence—then the throaty roar of the first engine as it bursts into life. And the squeal of rubber on asphalt as the car leaps forward, leaving an arc of black behind its spinning rear wheels. Contrasting with the utter stillness of a few seconds earlier, the air is choked with sound as the rest of the field stream past the pits and under the Dunlop

bridge, jockeying for position amongst themselves and hounding after the leader like a pack in full cry. The *Grand Prix d'Endurance* is on.'

So wrote Stirling Moss recently of that most dramatic motor-racing moment of the year—the start of the 24-Hour Race at Le Mans.

The motor racing tradition of Le Mans goes back to the dawn of the sport. For it was here, on a vast 65-mile circuit reaching far out into

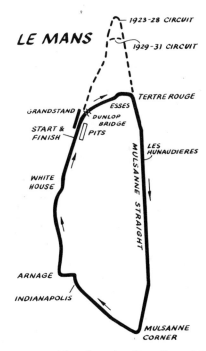

the countryside, that the first Grand Prix of all was run in 1906. Since then there have been several Le Mans circuits, each shorter than the one before, culminating in the present *Circuit Permanent de la Sarthe*, eight miles long, smooth as a billiard table and very, very fast. This circuit and its 24-Hour Race are probably the most famous in the world. Certainly none receives so much publicity. It is a unique event with a unique atmosphere of glamour and excitement.

But it is at night that Le Mans comes into

its own. Headlights stream past the brightly lit pit area. Out on the circuit there are fun fairs, cabarets, hot dog stands and a Hampstead Heath atmosphere. But the serious business of racing goes on and eyes grow bleary as dawn and its inevitable mist approach. For the few lucky ones, though, it all ends in triumph and rejoicing at 4 p.m. on Sunday afternoon. Yes, Le Mans is a must at least once in every enthusiast's life!

Lap Distance: 8·37 miles.

Location: Outside Le Mans, approximately 120 miles south-west of Paris.

Lap Record: Mike Hawthorn (4·1-litre Ferrari), 3 min. 58·7 sec., 126·15 m.p.h., during the 24-Hour race, June 1957.

Targa Florio

The Sicilian Targa Florio is the oldest race in the world run purely for sports cars. The series started in 1906 and is a Sports Car Championship event today.

Apart from half a dozen occasions when the race took the form of a circuit of the island of Sicily, and another four when it was held in a Palermo Park, the Targa Florio has always been held on one of the circuits which sound as though they were named after three of the Little Nigger Boys—Big Madonie, Medium Madonie and Short Madonie. Since 1951 the race's home ground has been the Short Madonie, although the adjective should be written 'short', for a single lap of it measures 45 miles!

This event, founded by Count Vincenzo Florio, is a tough battle over a tough course which winds into the rugged mountains of Sicily. There are barely four consecutive straight miles in its entire length, the other 41 miles being made up of nothing but corners. There are about 850 of them to each lap, or 20 per mile.

Lap Distance: 45 miles.

Location: Between Palermo and Messina, Sicily.

Lap Record: Stirling Moss (3-litre Aston Martin), 42 min. 17·5 sec., 63·42 m.p.h., during the Targa Florio, May 1958.

Sebring

The United States of America has two annual World Championship races. The first is at Sebring, in Florida, and counts for the Sports Car Championship, the second is at Indianapolis and comes into the Drivers' category.

The Indianapolis race is the traditional 500-mile event round the famous 'brickyard'. But the Sebring Twelve Hours Race, a kind of pint-sized Le Mans from 10 a.m. to 10 p.m., is a full-scale sports car event to European rules and regulations, run over an airfield circuit in Florida which, if not as perfectly surfaced as ours, is at least more hazardous so far as variety of corners is concerned.

Basically, Sebring is shaped like a right-angled triangle with long straights, tight corners and a quick right-left chicane. The main straight is over a mile long. But the infield section, much narrower than the rest, has several fast bends to help add speed and interest. A disadvantage of the circuit is that it is very much out in the wilds and a very long way from anywhere, though in that country of vast distances, people pop down to Sebring from, say, New York just as readily as we might pop up from London to Silverstone.

A great effort has been made recently to stage a full-scale Formula 1 Grand Prix of the United States at Sebring in December 1959.

Lap Distance: 5·2 miles.

Location: Florida, U.S.A.

Lap Record: Stirling Moss (3-litre Aston Martin), 3 min. 20·4 sec., 93·60 m.p.h., during 12-Hours Race, March 1958.

Massed crowds, flags and the hilltop castle mark the pit area of the Nürburgring and the start of the German Grand Prix

Lisbon

For some years Portugal has been a centre of motor racing and sports car Grands Prix have been held on the Vila Real circuit, on the Lisbon circuit and at Oporto, in the north of the country.

When, in 1958, Portugal was given the honour of holding its first World Championship Grand Prix, the event was held successfully on the Oporto road circuit. For 1959, however, the Grand Prix was transferred to the Lisbon circuit, the two cities taking turn and turn about as the race location.

The Lisbon track lies in the Monsanto Park, well within the boundaries of Portugal's capital city. It is $3\frac{1}{2}$ miles long and is composed principally of reasonably wide roads through typical, partly wooded parkland. At the time of writing the lap record stood at fractionally less than 90 m.p.h., this speed being set by a sports car as far back as 1957.

Lap Distance: 3.38 miles.

Location: Monsanto Park, Lisbon.

Lap Record: Masten Gregory (Ferrari Sports), 2 min. 16.1 sec., 89.3 m.p.h., during the Portuguese Grand Prix, June 1957.

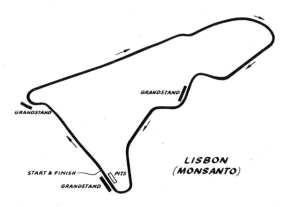

LISBON
(MONSANTO)

6 Rallies

RALLY driving is the world's most popular form of motoring sport. Rallies take place by the hundreds (by the thousand would hardly be an understatement in some cases) in every country where motorists get together and form a club. They come in every conceivable shape, size and form, from gigantic trans-continental events like the Algiers-Cape and Round Australia, to local club drives round the county on a Saturday afternoon. Somewhere between the two come the medium-distance 'classic' rallies of the European Rally Championship—events like the Monte Carlo, the Tulip and Sweden's romantically-named Rally to the Midnight Sun.

How rallying first started is difficult to say. At least we do know the game is just about as old as motoring itself. The first rally of all probably just happened, when a party of those intrepid automobilists of the early days decided to drive somewhere one day and give their run a competitive flavour by holding a test or two on the way. Anyway, the first large-scale rally in Great Britain was probably the famous 1,000 Mile Trial of 1900.

Since the war, and particularly in the last nine or ten years, the popularity of rally driving has soared to an all-time record level. Today the R.A.C. Fixture List notes not far short of 2,000 rallies held annually in Great Britain alone. Entries for the more popular events frequently exceed 150 cars, while even the smallest clubs can usually reckon on collecting forty to fifty competitors.

What is the reason for this 'rallymania'? Simply the ordinary man's love of making any hobby competitive, the great increase in car ownership and interest in motoring in recent years, and because the game is relatively cheap to play. Add to this the fact that the most unsuccessful driver in the oldest family saloon is a Fangio in his own eyes, and you have it.

Going rallying requires no special car, and it need cost little or nothing to convert the family runabout into a perfectly good vehicle for the job. Of course the more serious you are about rallying, or the more wealthy you are, the more you can spend if you want to.

You can spend a lot on improving the car's performance (if the regulations allow you to make mechanical modifications), and an absolute fortune on making it look like an accessory manufacturer's Christmas tree. On the other hand, quite important events have been won by perfectly ordinary cars straight off the family 'milk round'. And the writer, himself once started and finished a Monte

Competitor meets non-competitor on a mountain pass. A frequent rally hazard

The French couple Consten and Hébert who won the European Rally Championships on BP in 1958

Carlo Rally in a bread-and-butter vehicle, the total preparation of which amounted to one ordinary coal shovel for digging snow and a new set of plugs. We did not win any prizes, but we had a lot of fun. And, as with all sport, that is the main consideration.

European Rally Championship

Top title in the car rally world is that of European Rally Champion. This accolade does not carry as much public acclaim and prestige as the racing driving title, but there is little (if any) less merit to it. More so, in some ways, perhaps. For the top rally driver has to cover many thousands of miles of motoring in a year to get his honour. Motoring in all conditions—ice, snow, rain, fog and dust— over all kinds of roads from smooth, straight highways to twisting, unsurfaced mountain

passes. Moreover, virtually none of the rally roads are closed to other traffic when the competitors drive over them and practice to any great extent is impossible. The best that can be done by those drivers most intent on getting high in the results list is to make a reconnaissance of the route two or three weeks before the event. But sometimes the most thorough 'recce' is made useless, especially in winter, by a complete change in conditions by the time the rally starts. A couple of feet of snow can have fallen or melted, altering the whole complexion of things.

So the rally driver can never know exactly what awaits him in the next mile, or round the next bend for that matter. He may come sweeping round an ice-coated corner in the mountains, on the limits of adhesion and his time schedule, and find the whole road blocked by an unfortunate, ditched competitor, the local bus in difficulties, or even a horse and cart. Rally drivers' stories beginning 'We came round the corner and there it was . . .' would fill a larger book than this and are repeated *ad infinitum* over the beer glasses after every major event.

Perhaps the most famous of these tales concerns the driver ditched in the snow-bound mountains of the South of France on the last leg of a Monte Carlo Rally a few years ago. He and his long-suffering crew spent long hours digging out their large, heavy car. Then, just when they were about to regain the road, another competitor, late on schedule, came hurrying round the corner and slammed the first car right back where it came from!

The driver who manages to fight his way to the top of the Rally Championship, through the worst conditions of road and weather, must have with him a highly talented navigator/co-driver. His job is literally to keep his driver on the right track and take over the wheel so that No. 1 can have a rest. He need not be a virtuoso driver, but he must be competent enough to stay on the road and keep the place to which the maestro's skill has lifted them. Navigators sometimes have a recurrent nightmare in which they take over the wheel when their car is leading the rally and in sight of the finish. Then they put it straight into a ditch or a telegraph pole. The point in the dream where the No. 1 driver wakes up, is generally where the navigator wakes up in reality—screaming.

In these days of regularity sections, scores of miles which have to be covered at a precise, given average speed, not a decimal point either way, the navigator must also be something of a mathematical genius and a dab hand with a slide rule. In fact, the indirect responsibility resting on the shoulders of the navigator in modern Championship rallies to guide the car through, is almost

Victors Hébert and Consten with their Alfa Romeo Giulietta in a typical Alpine Rally setting

*Continental star
woman driver Annie Soisbault*

greater than that of the driver in driving it through.

The navigator moreover must be a master of tact, a skilled diplomat and be able to exert a soothing influence when temper and temperament shows itself—usually on the third night out in atrocious weather, when the driver's best laid plans seem to have gone slightly astray. More David-and-Jonathan friendships between driver and navigator have become irreparably shattered under such circumstances than from any other cause. 'I drove with him on that rally', they say of each other, 'and I have never spoken to him since!'

Pairing off for a major rally is one of the most difficult selection jobs in the world. And choosing a third crew member generally only complicates the issue. But a successful team who can work together one hundred per cent is often virtually unbeatable, and it pays them dividends to stick together rally after rally. For examples of this one has to look no further than the teams victorious in the Rally Championship in 1958—the French couple Hébert and Consten who won the title, and the British girls, Pat Moss and Ann Wisdom, who carried off the coveted Women's Championship against the strongest possible feminine opposition from the Continent.

The European Rally Championship consists of rallies run by nearly every European country this side of the Iron Curtain. And recently chinks have even appeared in the Curtain with such happenings as a Monte Carlo starting point in Warsaw, Poland. The events which counted for the Championship during 1959 were these:

18/25 January	Monte Carlo Rally (Monaco).
23/26 February	Sestrieres Rally (Italy).
27 April/2 May	Tulip Rally (Holland).
13/16 May	German Rally (Western Germany).
28/31 May	Acropolis Rally (Greece).
9/13 June	Rally to the Midnight Sun (Sweden).
23/30 June	Alpine Rally (France).
23/27 July	Adriatic Rally (Yugoslavia).

*European Women's Champions:
Ann Wisdom and Pat Moss*

Top British rally drivers Peter Harper and Peter Jopp display the silverware they won in the 1958 Alpine Rally

14/16 August	Rally of the Thousand Lakes (Finland).
2/6 September	Liège-Rome-Liège Rally (Belgium).
18/21 September	Viking Rally (Norway).
22/25 October	Iberian Rally (Portugal).
16/21 November	R.A.C. Rally (Great Britain).

The events for the Rally Championship 1960 are likely to be similar to those given above. The time of year at which the rallies take place remains fairly consistent from year to year, giving some idea of the weather conditions under which they are run.

The most famous of all the Rally Championship events is without doubt the Monte Carlo. The idea of several hundred motorists setting off in midwinter from starting points all over Europe and heading for the glamorous little principality on the Mediterranean coast catches the public imagination. And the imagination is assisted to a greater degree every ensuing year by the storm of publicity the rally attracts. They all come out for this one—press, television and film—and someone said of a recent 'Monte', when most of the runners fell snowbound by the wayside, there seemed to be more interviewers and photographers at the finish than there were drivers to be interviewed and photographed.

The 'Monte' can be extremely difficult, or it can be deceptively easy. It all depends on the weather. A foot or two of snow in the Massif Central, in the middle of France, and a few hundred miles of icy roads during this four-days-and-nights event can really sort out the sheep from the goats. On the other hand, a clear, snowless run, with perhaps only a little rain and fog to contend with, can mean that virtually everyone who started winds up in Monte Carlo at the finish with no loss of marks.

Sorting out a winner thus becomes no easy matter. Ideally, every rally should be won 'on the road'—the best driver over the two or three thousand mile route should head the list at the end. But only bad weather can really give the conditions in which the rally

Doing it the hard way; typical 'jungle' rally route in a marathon Australian event

maestro can show his worth. So the organizers are frequently reduced by sheer necessity to using various subterfuges in order to put into some sort of classification all those drivers who had finished the road section equal.

Several of the Championship rallies include driving tests along the road section route. Timed hillclimbs up various forbidding mountains (the Alps, French and Italian, are the favourites) and miniature races round the well-known circuits are two popular ways of 'sorting them out'. Brake and acceleration tests are also often used. But the Monte Carlo scheme is to include a regularity section either during the last stages of the rally, or as an addition to the principal road section. Latterly they have been included both during and after the event.

In 1959, for instance, the final classification test was run at night over a route of more than 250 miles in the Alpes Maritimes and included 'total regularity' sections in which the cars had to cover distances at precisely a given average speed. Penalty points were totted up at a rate of one per second if the car arrived more than ten seconds late at a control. And if they arrived early they could lose as many as 100 points. On top of all this, the competitors were told neither their route nor the average speed they were required to maintain until a few minutes before they set off on the run. The difficulties of such a test are, perhaps, not easy to appreciate. But averaging a set speed (always too high for comfortable driving under the conditions) between cunningly separated points, on narrow, twisting icy mountain roads, with perhaps fog and/or snow on the way, is no joke. And working out the averages on a piece of paper in a dark, jolting car is a complicated technical exercise on its own. Now it can be seen why the sensible rally driver employs a highly qualified mathematician to sit in the car with him.

Many people disapprove of the 'slide rule' aspect of modern rallies. The events, they say, should be won or lost on the road by the driver, not by a 'boffin' doing his sums in a back-seat 'office'. But with things as they are, it is difficult to see how this could be achieved. One event in the Rally Championship, though, is won or lost on the road and nowhere else.

When it first started several years ago, Belgium's contribution to the series, the Liège-Rome-Liège, lived up to its title and the rally route lay between these two cities. Nowadays it goes nowhere near Rome and the event is called the *Marathon de la Route*—but it still remains the toughest rally of the year.

Lasting four days and four nights, the Marathon covers nearly 3,500 miles in a single continuous stage of some 96 hours. There is no respite for the tired crews and the event is as near a week-long road race as a rally could ever be and still remain a rally. It is a supreme test of both driver, co-driver and car. Just to finish the Marathon is almost as great a feat of endurance and skill as winning any other lesser event outright. In 1958 only 22 crews out of a top-flight entry of 98 starters managed to complete the course through Germany, Yugoslavia, Italy, France and Belgium. Probably the most impressive performance was put up by the European Women Champions, Pat Moss and Ann Wisdom, who not only took the Ladies' Prize in an Austin-Healey 100-6, but also managed to finish fourth overall, the highest placing ever gained by a British entry. But without doubt the greatest Marathon performance of all was the late Johnny Claes's effort of a few years ago when the rally was still the Liège-Rome-Liège. Claes's co-driver became ill and the young Belgian drove the entire distance single-handed—and won.

Of the other Championship rallies, the most respected and best liked by the majority of drivers is the Alpine. This event wends its way over very nearly every mountain pass in the French, Italian and Swiss Alps, and a silver *Coupe des Alpes* for finishing the run with a 'clean sheet' is one of the most coveted awards in the whole of motoring sport.

The British contribution to the series, the R.A.C. Rally, has not as yet gained a particularly high international reputation and seldom attracts many entries from the rest of Europe. This is no reflection on the organizers but is largely due to the sheer impossibility of holding a real win-on-the-road rally within the confines of the British Isles. Consequently the road section is liberally sprinkled with driving tests which, in good weather, are likely to decide the whole outcome of the rally instead of just deciding ties and giving the road section survivors a final sorting out. In fact, no pretence is made about this, and the event is sub-titled 'The Rally of the Tests'. But driving tests by the handful are not popular on the Continent and, although there is no shortage of entrants from the home country, it remains really international in name only. However, the date for the 1959 R.A.C. Rally has been moved from March to late November and it is hoped that the weather conditions to be expected at that time of year will help to toughen up the event and give it a little more of the status it richly deserves.

As a general rule, first-class rally drivers do not make first-class racing drivers. In fact, few big names in the rally world have ever sat behind the wheel of a racing car at anything more than local speed event meetings. Conversely, not many top racing men have taken happily to rally driving. The techniques peculiar to each branch of the art are poles apart, and each needs its own particular approach. The most obvious exception proving this rule is, of course, the ever-versatile Stirling Moss. A few years ago Moss drove successfully in several Monte Carlo Rallies, and in the Alpine achieved the singular honour of winning the rarest of all rally trophies, an Alpine Cup in gold awarded for three penalty-free silver cup runs.

The Marathons

Out on their own in the rally world are the staggering trans-continental events which take place in and over some of the roughest and most inaccessible parts of the world.

There is the Algiers-Cape Rally, for instance, which traverses the length of Africa from the northern coast to the southernmost tip. It crosses the Sahara Desert, feels its way through the equatorial jungles and drives onwards over the dusty plains. The month-long 10,000-mile Round-Australia Rally literally encircles this vast continent, the cars having to drive over the most inhospitable terrain, on atrocious roads, and often in quite unspeakable weather conditions. They have to endure everything from ice, snow and freezing cold in the mountains to the scorching, searing heat of the desert. Then again, there is Kenya's annual rally, the Coronation Safari of over 3,000 miles, in which the British motor industry is taking an ever-increasing interest.

None of these events bears any relation or resemblance to rallies as we know them in Europe. Real roads, the tarmac-covered kind, are for the most part non-existent except in large towns. What is locally called a road is generally little more than a track through the wilderness that even the most adventurous mountain goat would regard with scorn. In dry weather they are rough, bumpy and so dusty that following another car is like driving through a thick, gritty fog. And after the slightest rainfall, they become a glue-like morass of mud in which the car often wallows helplessly like a washed-up whale.

The cars take the most brutal punishment imaginable, and although it often seems that they just cannot hold together under the strain, a surprising number of them survive the journey extremely well. And any car winning such an event is worthy of the highest praise, while the reward to its manufacturer is generally the highest sales. The public in the countries holding these marathons take great stock of their results, and even refrain from ordering a new car until the annual event has been run and won. This is especially true of the Coronation Safari. Here the competing cars have to be in absolutely standard order, so that the public know that whichever car wins, it will be identical to those sold in the local showrooms. Not a mechanically modified model whose closest resemblance to the 'shop' model is its shape, size and name.

Club Rallies

Rallies run by local motor clubs are Everyman's form of motoring sport. They take place by the score every week-end all over Great Britain and provide the easiest, cheapest and one of the most enjoyable means of active participation in competitive motoring. And you do not necessarily have to own a car to be able to join in. Local clubs are often short of good navigators, so if you specialize in this aspect of the game (and it is a specialist job these days) you will have a valuable service to offer the car driving members.

Club rallies take place by day and by night, in summer and winter, over long distances and short and are all graded by the R.A.C. according to their status. At one end of the scale are the events with National status, open to any holder of an R.A.C. competition licence valid for the event. Three well-known examples are the Thames Estuary Motor Club's 'Cat's Eyes' Rally, the London Motor Club's London Rally and the Midland Automobile Club's 'Birmingham Post' Rally. Incidentally, these together with several other rallies run in various parts of Great Britain, count towards the annually awarded R.A.C. Rally Championship.

All these bigger events cover at least two days and a night, some considerably more, and are heavily supported. Often the entry lists are over-subscribed and many would-be entrants have to be reluctantly turned away. The routes cover many hundreds of miles through the remoter parts of the country, and it is amazing just how remote the Welsh mountains, the Pennines and even Romney Marsh on the Kent coast can be in the middle of a wet, foggy or icy winter's night. The accent is laid heavily on navigating, time-keeping and the maintenance of set average speeds, and there is invariably a driving test or two either on the way or at the end. National rallies may not last as long as the big Rally Championship ones, but in their own way they are often every bit as exacting and exhausting.

In the middle classification come the rallies with Restricted status. There are considerably more of these, and they are open to members of the organizing club, plus the members of any other clubs which the organizers may care to invite along to take part. The number of invited clubs, incidentally, is limited to ten—a round robin cannot be sent out to every club in the book, or this would destroy the object of the status and turn every Restricted event into a virtually National one. Restricted rallies frequently last two days, or at least a night with an afternoon and a morning tacked on to each end.

Finally, there are the Closed status rallies in which only members of the organizing club are allowed to take part. These form the vast majority of events in the R.A.C. Fixture List and despite their being organized on a small scale, many of them achieve a standard of efficiency and excellence which would be admired in far more ambitious rallies. Some of them last two days but most are confined to a single day or night and cover a modest mileage. But they have all the ingredients of the large-scale events and provide one of the best ways of all for 'first-timers' to find out what the game is all about.

7 Facts and Figures

The tables of race results contained in this chapter are reproduced from THE MOTOR REFERENCE YEAR BOOK 1959, *by courtesy of the publishers, Temple Press Limited*

WORLD CHAMPIONSHIP OF DRIVERS

THE Drivers' World Championship as it is today was instituted in 1950. The title goes to the driver making the six best performances in the annual series of Grands Prix known as the Grandes Épreuves, plus certain other races chosen for their importance (see Chapter 1, p. 20). No other races count.

The championship marking system rewards a consistently high standard of driving throughout the season. The driver who wins the most Grandes Épreuves does not necessarily become World Champion. An example of this occurred in 1958 when Mike Hawthorn, after winning only one race in the series, gained the title from Stirling Moss, who won four of them. Hawthorn amassed points by consistent high placing and a string of fastest laps.

Miracle man of the World Championship is the Argentinian star, now retired, Juan Manuel Fangio, who won the title five times driving four different makes of car.

1950	G. Farina, Italy (Alfa Romeo)
1951	J. M. Fangio, Argentine (Alfa Romeo)
1952	A. Ascari, Italy (Ferrari)
1953	A. Ascari, Italy (Ferrari)
1954	J. M. Fangio, Argentine (Maserati and Mercedes-Benz)
1955	J. M. Fangio, Argentine (Mercedes-Benz)
1956	J. M. Fangio, Argentine (Ferrari)
1957	J. M. Fangio, Argentine (Maserati)
1958	J. M. Hawthorn, Great Britain (Ferrari)

RESULTS OF THE GRANDES ÉPREUVES
The French Grand Prix

The French Grand Prix, or to give it its proper title, the Grand Prix of the Automobile Club of France, was the first of all Grands Prix. For many years it was the only Grand Prix of the season, and even in these days of equality between World Championship events, it is still considered by many to be the most important of all. The race has been held on circuits all over France, varying in length from the 65 miles of the original Le Mans circuit in 1906 to the bare five, but very fast, miles of the present track at Rheims. The results of the French

Grand Prix tell the story of big-time motor racing, illustrating the development of the Grand Prix car from the earliest days to the present time. In nearly every case, the winner of this race has been 'car of the year'.

Year	Circuit	Driver	Car	Speed
1906	Le Mans	Szisz	12·8-litre Renault	63·86 m.p.h.
1907	Dieppe	Nazarro	15-litre Fiat	70·60 m.p.h.
1908	Dieppe	Lautenschlager	13-litre Mercedes	68·90 m.p.h.
1909–11	No race			
1912	Dieppe	G. Boillot	7·6-litre Peugeot	63·30 m.p.h.
1913	Amiens	G. Boillot	5·6-litre Peugeot	72·13 m.p.h.
1914	Lyons	Lautenschlager	4·5-litre Mercedes	63·30 m.p.h.
1915–20	No race			
1921	Le Mans	Murphy	3-litre Duesenburg	79·04 m.p.h.
1922	Strasbourg	Nazarro	2-litre Fiat	79·33 m.p.h.
1923	Tours	Segrave	2-litre Sunbeam	75·45 m.p.h.
1924	Lyons	Campari	2-litre Alfa Romeo	70·96 m.p.h.
1925	Montlhéry	Benoist-Divo	2-litre Delage	77·20 m.p.h.
1926	Miramas	Goux	1½-litre Bugatti	68·00 m.p.h.
1927	Montlhéry	Benoist	1½-litre Delage	77·20 m.p.h.
1928	Comminges	Williams	2·3-litre Bugatti	80·68 m.p.h.
1929	Le Mans	Williams	2·3-litre Bugatti	82·59 m.p.h.
1930	Pau	Etancelin	2-litre Bugatti	90·10 m.p.h.
1931	Montlhéry	Chiron-Varzi	2·3-litre Bugatti	78·07 m.p.h.
1932	Rheims	Nuvolari	2·6-litre Alfa Romeo	92·32 m.p.h.
1933	Montlhéry	Campari	2·9-litre Maserati	81·49 m.p.h.
1934	Montlhéry	Chiron	2·9-litre Alfa Romeo	85·06 m.p.h.
1935	Montlhéry	Caracciola	3·9-litre Mercedes-Benz	77·40 m.p.h.
1936	Montlhéry	Wimille-Sommer	3·3-litre Bugatti	79·71 m.p.h.
1937	Montlhéry	Chiron	4-litre Talbot-Darracq	82·48 m.p.h.
1938	Rheims	von Brauchitsch	3-litre Mercedes-Benz	101·30 m.p.h.
1939	Rheims	Müller	3-litre Auto-Union	105·25 m.p.h.
1940–46	No race			
1947	Lyons	Chiron	4·5-litre Talbot-Darracq	78·10 m.p.h.
1948	Rheims	Wimille	1½-litre Alfa Romeo	102·10 m.p.h.
1949	Comminges	Pozzi	3·5-litre Delahaye	87·94 m.p.h.
1950	Rheims	Fangio	1½-litre Alfa Romeo	104·83 m.p.h.
1951	Rheims	Fangio	1½-litre Alfa Romeo	110·97 m.p.h.
1952	Rouen	Ascari	2-litre Ferrari	80·14 m.p.h.
1953	Rheims	Hawthorn	2-litre Ferrari	113·65 m.p.h.
1954	Rheims	Fangio	2·5-litre Mercedes-Benz	115·67 m.p.h.
1955	No race			
1956	Rheims	Collins	2·5-litre Ferrari-Lancia	122·21 m.p.h.
1957	Rouen	Fangio	2·5-litre Maserati	100·02 m.p.h.
1958	Rheims	Hawthorn	2·5-litre Ferrari	125·46 m.p.h.

NOTE: The 1928, 1936, 1937 and 1949 races were for sports cars.

The Italian Grand Prix

With only four exceptions, the Italian Grand Prix has always been held on the Monza circuit outside Milan, though the track itself has been altered considerably on several occasions.

Nowadays the race, held in September, forms the climax of the Grand Prix season. It is the last of the series to take place in Europe, the weather is usually perfect for the game and the closely matched high speed battles which occur each year are the very essence of motor racing.

Year	Circuit	Driver	Car	Speed
1921	Brescia	Goux	3-litre Ballot	90·40 m.p.h.
1922	Monza	Bordino	2-litre Fiat	86·89 m.p.h.
1923	Monza	Salamano	2-litre Fiat	91·06 m.p.h.
1924	Monza	Ascari	2-litre Alfa Romeo	98·76 m.p.h.
1925	Monza	Brilli-Peri	2-litre Alfa Romeo	94·76 m.p.h.
1926	Monza	'Sabipa'	1½-litre Bugatti	85·87 m.p.h.
1927	Monza	Benoist	1½-litre Delage	90·04 m.p.h.
1928	Monza	Chiron	2·3-litre Bugatti	99·14 m.p.h.
1929	No race			
1930	No race			
1931	Monza	Campari and Nuvolari	2·3-litre Alfa Romeo	96·17 m.p.h.
1932	Monza	Campari and Nuvolari	2·6-litre Alfa Romeo	104·13 m.p.h.
1933	Monza	Fagioli	2·6-litre Alfa Romeo	108·58 m.p.h.
1934	Monza	Caracciola and Fagioli	3·9-litre Mercedes-Benz	65·30 m.p.h.
1935	Monza	Stuck	5-litre Auto-Union	85·17 m.p.h.
1936	Monza	Rosemeyer	6-litre Auto-Union	84·10 m.p.h.
1937	Leghorn	Caracciola	5·6-litre Mercedes-Benz	81·59 m.p.h.
1938	Monza	Nuvolari	3-litre Auto-Union	96·70 m.p.h.
1939–46	No race			
1947	Milan	Trossi	1½-litre Alfa Romeo	70·29 m.p.h.
1948	Turin	Wimille	1½-litre Alfa Romeo	70·38 m.p.h.
1949	Monza	Ascari	4½-litre Ferrari	105·09 m.p.h.
1950	Monza	Farina	1½-litre Alfa Romeo	109·67 m.p.h.
1951	Monza	Ascari	4½-litre Ferrari	115·53 m.p.h.
1952	Monza	Ascari	2-litre Ferrari	109·80 m.p.h.
1953	Monza	Fangio	2-litre Maserati	110·69 m.p.h.
1954	Monza	Fangio	2½-litre Mercedes-Benz	111·99 m.p.h.
1955	Monza	Fangio	2½-litre Mercedes-Benz	128·50 m.p.h.
1956	Monza	Moss	2½-litre Maserati	129·75 m.p.h.
1957	Monza	Moss	2½-litre Vanwall	120·30 m.p.h.
1958	Monza	Brooks	2½-litre Vanwall	121·17 m.p.h.

The Belgian Grand Prix

Third oldest of the Grandes Épreuves still being run is the Belgian Grand Prix, held, with a single exception, on the magnificent Spa circuit. The race usually takes place during the first half of June, and in 1958 achieved the distinction of being the fastest World Championship event ever run.

Year	Circuit	Drivers	Car	Speed
1925	Spa	Ascari	2-litre Alfa Romeo	74·36 m.p.h.
1926–9	No Race			
1930	Spa	Chiron	2·3-litre Bugatti	72·10 m.p.h.
1931	Spa	Williams and Conelli	2·3-litre Bugatti	82·01 m.p.h.
1932	No race			
1933	Spa	Nuvolari	2·9-litre Maserati	89·23 m.p.h.
1934	Spa	Dreyfus	3·5-litre Bugatti	86·91 m.p.h.

Year	Circuit	Drivers	Car	Speed
1935	Spa	Caracciola	3·9-litre Mercedes-Benz	97·87 m.p.h.
1936	No race			
1937	Spa	Hasse	6-litre Auto-Union	104·07 m.p.h.
1938	No race			
1939	Spa	Lang	3-litre Mercedes-Benz	94·39 m.p.h.
1940–45	No race			
1946	Brussels	Chaboud	4½-litre Delahaye	67·07 m.p.h.
1947	Spa	Wimille	1½-litre Alfa Romeo	95·28 m.p.h.
1948	No race			
1949	Spa	Rosier	4½-litre Talbot-Darracq	96·95 m.p.h.
1950	Spa	Fangio	1½-litre Alfa Romeo	110·05 m.p.h.
1951	Spa	Farina	1½-litre Alfa Romeo	114·26 m.p.h.
1952	Spa	Ascari	2-litre Ferrari	103·13 m.p.h.
1953	Spa	Ascari	2-litre Ferrari	112·47 m.p.h.
1954	Spa	Fangio	2½-litre Maserati	115·08 m.p.h.
1955	Spa	Fangio	2½-litre Mercedes-Benz	118·84 m.p.h.
1956	Spa	Collins	2½-litre Ferrari-Lancia	118·43 m.p.h.
1957	No race			
1958	Spa	Brooks	2½-litre Vanwall	129·93 m.p.h.

The German Grand Prix

The first German Grand Prix was held on the Avus circuit in the suburbs of Berlin and returned there in 1959. For the intervening thirty years the scene of the race was the fabulous Nürburgring, south of Cologne, and the event itself is the World Championship's outstanding test of sheer driving skill. Only drivers of the very highest class have ever won.

Year	Circuit	Drivers	Car	Speed
1926	Avus	Caracciola	7-litre Mercedes-Benz	84·50 m.p.h.
1927	Nürburgring	Merz	7-litre Mercedes-Benz	63·75 m.p.h.
1928	Nürburgring	Caracciola and Werner	7-litre Mercedes-Benz	64·60 m.p.h.
1929	Nürburgring	Chiron	2·3-litre Bugatti	66·79 m.p.h.
1930	No race			
1931	Nürburgring	Caracciola	7-litre Mercedes-Benz	67·29 m.p.h.
1932	Nürburgring	Caracciola	2·6-litre Alfa Romeo	74·13 m.p.h.
1933	No race			
1934	Nürburgring	Stuck	4·4-litre Auto-Union	75·14 m.p.h.
1935	Nürburgring	Nuvolari	3·8-litre Alfa Romeo	75·25 m.p.h.
1936	Nürburgring	Rosemeyer	6-litre Auto-Union	81·80 m.p.h.
1937	Nürburgring	Caracciola	5·6-litre Mercedes-Benz	82·77 m.p.h.
1938	Nürburgring	Seaman	3-litre Mercedes-Benz	80·75 m.p.h.
1939	Nürburgring	Caracciola	3-litre Mercedes-Benz	75·18 m.p.h.
1940–49	No race			
1950	Nürburgring	Ascari	2-litre Ferrari	77·67 m.p.h.
1951	Nürburgring	Ascari	4½-litre Ferrari	83·76 m.p.h.
1952	Nürburgring	Ascari	2-litre Ferrari	82·21 m.p.h.
1953	Nürburgring	Farina	2-litre Ferrari	83·89 m.p.h.
1954	Nürburgring	Fangio	2½-litre Mercedes-Benz	82·77 m.p.h.
1955	No race			
1956	Nürburgring	Fangio	2½-litre Ferrari-Lancia	85·57 m.p.h.
1957	Nürburgring	Fangio	2½-litre Maserati	88·79 m.p.h.
1958	Nürburgring	Brooks	2½-litre Vanwall	90·35 m.p.h.

The British Grand Prix

The first British Grand Prix was held at Brooklands in 1926. It was won by a Delage, the drivers of which had to keep calling at the pits during the race to bathe their feet in a bucket of water because the car's exhaust system burned them! During the 1930s, the Donington Grand Prix became Britain's major motor racing event. This race was never officially recognized as the British Grand Prix. However, as it was the Grand Prix in everything but name, the results are given here for the record.

Year	Circuit	Driver	Car	Speed
1926	Brooklands	Senéchal and Wagner	1½-litre Delage	71·61 m.p.h.
1927	Brooklands	Benoist	1½-litre Delage	85·59 m.p.h.
1928–34	No Race			
1935	Donington	Shuttleworth	2·9-litre Alfa Romeo	63·97 m.p.h.
1936	Donington	Ruesch and Seaman	2·8-litre Alfa Romeo	69·23 m.p.h.
1937	Donington	Rosemeyer	6-litre Auto-Union	82·85 m.p.h.
1938	Donington	Nuvolari	3-litre Auto-Union	80·49 m.p.h.
1939–48	No Race			
1949	Silverstone	de Graffenried	1½-litre Maserati	77·31 m.p.h.
1950	Silverstone	Farina	1½-litre Alfa Romeo	90·95 m.p.h.
1951	Silverstone	Gonzales	4½-litre Ferrari	96·11 m.p.h.
1952	Silverstone	Ascari	2-litre Ferrari	90·92 m.p.h.
1953	Silverstone	Ascari	2-litre Ferrari	92·97 m.p.h.
1954	Silverstone	Gonzales	2½-litre Ferrari	89·69 m.p.h.
1955	Aintree	Moss	2½-litre Mercedes-Benz	86·47 m.p.h.
1956	Silverstone	Fangio	2½-litre Ferrari-Lancia	98·65 m.p.h.
1957	Aintree	Brooks and Moss	2½-litre Vanwall	86·80 m.p.h.
1958	Silverstone	Collins	2½-litre Ferrari	102·05 m.p.h.

The Monaco Grand Prix

The Monaco 'round the houses' Grand Prix is the slowest of the World Championship series. It is also one of the most spectacular and the most interesting. Firstly because it is held in the delightful surroundings of Monte Carlo in springtime, secondly because sheer lack of room in which to overdo things makes it the easiest job in the world for the driver to bounce his car off a solid stone wall, or as on one occasion (Ascari in 1955), go straight into the harbour. Adeptness at avoiding other crashed cars is frequently a major qualification for winning this race.

Year	Circuit	Driver	Car	Speed
1929	Monte Carlo	Williams	2·3-litre Bugatti	49·83 m.p.h.
1930	Monte Carlo	Dreyfus	2·3-litre Bugatti	53·63 m.p.h.
1931	Monte Carlo	Chiron	2·3-litre Bugatti	54·09 m.p.h.
1932	Monte Carlo	Nuvolari	2·3-litre Alfa Romeo	55·80 m.p.h.
1933	Monte Carlo	Varzi	2·3-litre Bugatti	57·04 m.p.h.
1934	Monte Carlo	Moll	2·6-litre Alfa Romeo	55·86 m.p.h.
1935	Monte Carlo	Fagioli	4-litre Mercedes-Benz	58·17 m.p.h.
1936	Monte Carlo	Caracciola	4·7-litre Mercedes-Benz	51·69 m.p.h.
1937	Monte Carlo	von Brauchitsch	5·6-litre Mercedes-Benz	63·27 m.p.h.
1938–47	No race			

Year	Circuit	Driver	Car	Speed
1948	Monte Carlo	Farina	1½-litre Maserati	59·61 m.p.h.
1949	No race			
1950	Monte Carlo	Fangio	1½-litre Alfa Romeo	61·33 m.p.h.
1951	No race			
1952	Monte Carlo	V. Marzotto	2·7-litre Ferrari	58·20 m.p.h.
1953	No race			
1954	No race			
1955	Monte Carlo	Trintignant	2½-litre Ferrari	65·80 m.p.h.
1956	Monte Carlo	Moss	2½-litre Maserati	64·94 m.p.h.
1957	Monte Carlo	Fangio	2½-litre Maserati	64·75 m.p.h.
1958	Monte Carlo	Trintignant	2-litre Cooper	67·98 m.p.h.

NOTE: The 1952 race was for sports cars.

The Dutch Grand Prix

The Dutch Grand Prix joined the motor racing calendar in 1949 though it did not gain World Championship status immediately. It was held on the then newly constructed Zandvoort circuit. The 1954 event was for sports cars, run in two heats and a final, and did not count for the World Championship. For financial reasons there was no race in 1956 or 1957.

Year	Circuit	Driver	Car	Speed
1949	Zandvoort	Villoresi	1½-litre Ferrari	77·12 m.p.h.
1950	Zandvoort	Rosier	4½-litre Talbot-Darracq	76·44 m.p.h.
1951	Zandvoort	Rosier	4½-litre Talbot-Darracq	78·46 m.p.h.
1952	Zandvoort	Ascari	2-litre Ferrari	81·15 m.p.h.
1953	Zandvoort'	Ascari	2-litre Ferrari	81·04 m.p.h.
1954	Zandvoort	Brown	2-litre Cooper-Bristol	
1955	Zandvoort	Fangio	2½-litre Mercedes-Benz	89·62 m.p.h.
1956	No race			
1957	No race			
1958	Zandvoort	Moss'	2½-litre Vanwall	93·96 m.p.h.

The Moroccan Grand Prix

The first Moroccan race to count for the World Championship took place at Casablanca in 1957. The event is held in North African sunshine in October. It is the last of the annual series of Grandes Épreuves and achieved considerable importance in 1958 as the deciding event in the World Championship battle between Mike Hawthorn and Stirling Moss.

Year	Circuit	Driver	Car	Speed
1957	Casablanca	Behra	2½-litre Maserati	112·65 m.p.h.
1958	Casablanca	Moss	2½-litre Vanwall	116·22 m.p.h.

The Portuguese Grand Prix

Latest arrival on the World Championship scene is the Grand Prix of Portugal. The circuit used for the 1958 event was in the suburbs of Oporto, in the northern part of the country, where one of·the major hazards was the presence of tramlines and cobble-stones made greasy by pre-race drizzle. In 1959 the race was moved to the Monsanto circuit outside Lisbon, scene of sports car Grands Prix in recent years.

Year	Circuit	Driver	Car	Speed
1958	Oporto	Moss	2½-litre Vanwall	104·90 m.p.h.

The Grand Prix of Europe

Each year one of the Grandes Épreuves is given the additional title of European Grand Prix. The race keeps its national title as well and the winners given below can be found, in fact, in the foregoing lists under their appropriate Grands Prix. World Championship markings stay the same, the only difference between the European event and the others in the calendar being one of prestige.

Year	Circuit	Driver	Car	Speed
1923	Monza	Salamano	2-litre Fiat	91·06 m.p.h.
1924	Lyons	Campari	2-litre Alfa Romeo	70·96 m.p.h.
1925	Spa	Ascari, Antonio	2-litre Alfa Romeo	74·36 m.p.h.
1926	San Sebastian	Goux	1½-litre Bugatti	76·40 m.p.h.
1927	Monza	Benoist	1½-litre Delage	90·04 m.p.h.
1928	Monza	Chiron	2·3-litre Bugatti	99·14 m.p.h.
1929	No race			
1930	Spa	Chiron	2·3-litre Bugatti	72·10 m.p.h.
1931–46	No race			
1947	Spa	Wimille	1½-litre Alfa Romeo	95·28 m.p.h.
1948	Berne	Trossi	1½-litre Alfa Romeo	90·81 m.p.h.
1949	Monza	Ascari, Alberto	1½-litre Ferrari	105·09 m.p.h.
1950	Silverstone	Farina	1½-litre Alfa Romeo	90·95 m.p.h.
1951	Rheims	Fangio	1½-litre Alfa Romeo	110·97 m.p.h.
1952	Spa	Ascari, Alberto	2-litre Ferrari	103·13 m.p.h.
1953	No race			
1954	Nürburgring	Fangio	2½-litre Mercedes-Benz	82·77 m.p.h.
1955	Monaco	Trintignant	2½-litre Ferrari	65·80 m.p.h.
1956	Monza	Moss	2½-litre Maserati	129·75 m.p.h.
1957	Aintree	Brooks and Moss	2½-litre Vanwall	86·80 m.p.h.
1958	Spa	Brooks	2½-litre Vanwall	129·93 m.p.h.

CLASSIC SPORTS CAR RACES

The Mille Miglia

Regarded by many as the greatest race of the year, by others as sheer madness, Italy's thousand-mile race followed a tradition set by the famous city-to-city races of sixty years ago. Brescia-Ravenna-Pescara-Rome-Florence-Bologna-Mantua-Brescia the route ran—a giant oblong course over every kind of road, from fast, flat, almost endless straights to winding mountain passes. And during the race much of it was open to normal traffic as well, not to mention the added hazard of the thousands of spectators who crowded in on each side, and whose prime joy was to see just how close they could get to cars travelling at 100 m.p.h. without being touched. Eventually, the crisis came in 1957 when the Ferrari driven by the Marquis de Portago crashed less than 50 miles from the finish, killing several spectators. The

Mille Miglia was banned and has not been held since, although to keep the name alive it was given to a minor rally-type of event bearing no resemblance to the race.

The Targo Florio

The Targo Florio shares with the French Grand Prix the honour of being the oldest classic motor race still in the calendar. It is held annually in Sicily and counts towards the World Sports Car Championship. The race started its long life on the 90-mile Big Madonie circuit. On six occasions it took the form of a 650-mile drive round Sicily. For many years it was run over the 67-mile Medium Madonie circuit, and four times just before the war it went to Favorita Park in Palermo, where it became just another motor race and not a particularly good one either. Since 1951, the Targo Florio has settled down on the 45-mile Short Madonie circuit.

The Le Mans 24-Hour Race

The most famous and the most widely publicised motor race of the year is the 24-hour Grand Prix of Endurance at Le Mans. Whether it is over-rated, or whether it really is the best race of the year is a matter of personal opinion. From the point of view of many drivers, however, it is not popular as it lets loose on the circuit over fifty cars of all shapes and sizes, the 'tiddlers' often getting in the way of the bigger machinery travelling at almost twice the speed. On the other hand, for the spectator (given fine weather) Le Mans, with its racing round the clock, is an exciting spectacle which can be seen nowhere else. Some return year after year, others say that if you have seen one, you have seen them all. That, too, is a matter of opinion. However, British cars have done well at Le Mans, the fame and fortune attaching to the race in recent years being almost a monopoly of Jaguar.

Run concurrently with the scratch race, the Grand Prix of Endurance (awarded to the car covering the greatest distance in the 24 hours), is the Index of Performance. This is a handicap race, each car being given a set distance to cover within the 24 hours, according to its engine size. Both races are ostensibly of equal importance and the prize money for each is the same.

The Tourist Trophy

This race is older even than the French Grand Prix, and although it is now for sports rather than touring cars, it has a greater claim than any other to being Britain's classic event. Like the motor cycle T.T., the Tourist Trophy started on the Isle of Man. Unlike the two-wheel race, though, it moved after its pioneering days to the 13-mile Ards circuit in Northern Ireland, where it remained for nine years. Then following an accident involving spectators in the 1936 race, it moved once more, to Donington. After the war, the Tourist Trophy returned to Northern Ireland, to the excellent $7\frac{1}{2}$-mile Dundrod circuit. Here, in 1950, Stirling Moss scored his first big victory in the teeming rain characteristic of so many Dundrod races. After five races at Dundrod, and a major collision in the last of them, the circuit was deemed unsuitable for modern super high performance machinery. Consequently in 1958 the Tourist Trophy moved again, this time to Goodwood.

The World's Land Speed Record

From 39 m.p.h. in a car propelled by electricity in 1898, to 394 m.p.h. in one propelled by two huge aircraft engines in 1947—that is the story of less than fifty years' progress in the history of automobile engineering and man's quest for speed. For the World's Land Speed Record has attracted man like the peak of Everest or the depths of the ocean. But the ultimate limits of speed are infinite, bounded only by man's ability to reach them. Already efforts are being made to travel still faster over the magic measured mile. In the near future, Donald Campbell hopes to reach 450 m.p.h., perhaps 500 m.p.h., with his new turbo-jet car. As methods of propulsion progress, so also do the figures for the fastest on earth.

The B.R.D.C. Gold Star

Top British motor-racing honour is the Gold Star awarded annually by the British Racing Drivers Club, the club of which membership itself can be gained only by earning it on the race track. The Gold Star is awarded on a somewhat complicated marking system which takes into account World Championship events (Drivers' and Sports Car) and other International and National races in the sporting calendar, marks for the latter categories varying according to the length of the race in question. Additional Gold Stars can be awarded to members at the discretion of the B.R.D.C. Committee for outstanding achievements in motoring sport. Thus, Mike Hawthorn received one in 1958 for winning the World Championship, in addition to Stirling Moss, who headed the list so far as marks were concerned. Moss, indeed, has made a habit of heading the list in recent years—he has collected eight stars between 1950 and 1958.

INTERNATIONAL FLAG SIGNALS

RED: Race to stop at once.

YELLOW, waved: Great danger. Be prepared to stop.

YELLOW, held steady: Be careful. Danger.

BLUE, waved: Another driver is trying to overtake you.

BLUE, held steady: Another driver is close behind you.

YELLOW with RED stripes: Be careful. There is oil on the circuit.

WHITE: An ambulance or official car is on the circuit.

BLACK with WHITE number: Car bearing that number to stop at its pit after the next lap.

NATIONAL FLAG: Start of race.

BLACK and WHITE chequered: End of race.

3